THE EFFENDI
AND THE
PREGNANT POT

— Uygur Folktales from China

Translated by

Primerose Gigliesi
and
Robert C. Friend

NEW WORLD PRESS

Beijing, China

Cover painting and illustrations by Li Shan
Cover design by Wu Shousong

Published by:
NEW WORLD PRESS
24 Baiwanzhuang Road,
Beijing, China

Distributed by:
CHINA PUBLICATIONS CENTRE
(GUOJI SHUDIAN)
P.O. Box 399, Beijing, China

Printed in the People's Republic of China

CONTENTS

PREFACE

These droll satirical stories belong to the folktale heritage of the Uygurs, a Muslim minority nationality numbering some seven million who inhabit Xinjiang (Sinkiang) in northwest China. It is a land of towering snow-capped mountains around the edge of one of worst deserts in the world, a land of herding and oasis agriculture.

The tales are also part of the oral folklore of the entire Muslim world. They are the result of that strange and wonderful capacity of stories to pass from person to person, travel from one country to another and, over the centuries, to spread to entire continents.

The Uygurs are the descendents of the ancient Huihe. Their language belongs to the Turkic branch of the Altaic language family. During the period from the 6th to the 8th centuries, the Huihes were under the domination of the Tu-jue (Turki) Khanate, which at its height claimed power from Mongolia to the Caspian. In the 9th century, the Huihes succeeded in establishing two independent kingdoms (khanates), one in Gansu and the other in Xinjiang.

The hero of these tales is the Effendi Nasreddin. Effendi in Uygur was a title originally given to a person of high culture or social status. Now, in the Uygur tradition the title has become almost a personal name. The Chinese version of these Uygur stories, where the term *effendi* is transliterated with three Chinese characters pronounced "*ah fan ti*", echoes this.

Tradition presents the Effendi Nasreddin as a legendary figure, perhaps based on a historical person. We meet him in satirical tales all over the far-flung Muslim world. In the Urdu tradition he is the *Mullah.* Among the Uzbek people he is the hero of a certain type of *dastan* (story). He is known among the Tadjiks, Afghans, Persians, Azerbaijanians, Turks, and practically to all the peoples of Central Asia and the Eastern Mediterranian world.

Our motive in introducing this collection of Uygur tales of the Effendi Nasreddin came from the need to underline why this folk hero — so deeply engrained in the folklore of the Muslim peoples and loved by the Uygur minority — has become a beloved and familiar figure throughout China. Translations of his tales have gone through many printings.

Until a few years ago, we did not even know of the existence of Nasreddin. We were captured by his audacious character in a totally unexpected way. A young Chinese attendant in the hotel where we live in Beijing first mentioned Nasreddin to us. He had a small book in his hand and was reading it avidly and with obvious enjoyment. Curious, we read the first tale, then the second, the third, the fourth. We were unable to stop. We began to translate them at first for sheer amusement. Their subtle, stinging, dry humor was so real that one could almost touch it. We did not realize that we were being drawn little by little into a work which would later require of us something more than curiosity and enthusiasm. We were dealing with a new facet of modern Chinese literature.

We began mentioning "Afanti", the Effendi Nasreddin, to Chinese people, only to discover that everyone we talked with, including children, knew the figure and the tales. Our interest then became intense and we began in earnest to question everyone we met, including people from many different countries. Thus, this work was not born in the scholarly silence of a library, although, of course, we have worked with specialized research material. It was born in long talks with the most varied people, Chinese and others, a large number of whom were of Muslim background. These conversations gradually framed the story of Nasreddin as colorfully as a large mosaic.

It is not important to establish whether these tales circulated in old China before the founding of the People's Republic in 1949. What is significant is that in New China they have been published and republished and have become a valuable means of education. The Nasreddin who has entered the hearts of the Chinese people conveys a message: the bullying of feudal rulers; their abuse of authority; the stupidity and immorality of the powerful; the hatred, scorn, lack of respect which the oppressed feel toward all tyrants; and the humor and wisdom of the poor.

What strikes the reader at once is not the inevitability of Nasreddin's victory. It is the fact that his wise and crafty humor never amuses or entertains the rich person, lord, or padishah. Certainly his *The Goose with One Leg* reminds the reader of Boccaccio's *Chichibio e la Gru* (Chichibio and the Crane). But when Chichibio tries to convince his master, Currado, that cranes "have not but one thigh and one leg", the ire of the noble lord collapses into fits of laughter. The reaction of the padishah toward Nasreddin is completely different. When the effendi eats a leg of the roast goose, the padishah is not at all amused or benevolent. Nor does the effendi toady to the rich and powerful as Chichibio, "the Venetian liar", does to Currado.

Most of the time, the lords become angry with the

effendi but do not punish him. They let him go without saying a word, not because they accept their defeat at his hands or feel inclined to be lenient with him, but because between them and Nasreddin there is an irreconcilable contradiction of which they are fully aware. At times the stories seem to take place in an atmosphere of calm, but it is a deceptive calm used only to hide the internal passions and the ideological clash of the antagonists.

The Effendi Nasreddin is a common man, intelligent, courageous and of a character who fights back. He is essentially a worker, a poor man, even if at times his social condition seems different and we find him at the court of the padishah or in the houses of the rich. In fact, the starting point of many of his tales is often hunger or, in any case, poverty. *The Three Truths, The Glutton* and *The Rolls and the Padishah* are cases in point. The moral is always the same: the victory of Nasreddin over the cadi, the official, the imam, the rich lord, the padishah, and even Allah. We can say the same for *The Trial, The Mutton Bone, The Clothes of the Guest, The Bag of Tricks* and *The Miracle*.

The effendi is a man who revolts in his own particular way. The effendi exposes, condemns and fights the concept of the world held by the ruling class. The effendi is the poor man whom the ruling class knows it must weigh and measure carefully because he is not an isolated individual and his ideology is not a subjective, arbitrary fact but a far more general phenomenon.

Thus, Nasreddin is not an exception among men, not the primary figure in the foreground who contrasts with the general mediocrity and coarseness. He is linked with the simple people by warm and strong ties. *The Gold Plant, A Dinner of Smells,* and *The Thing Which Is Eaten*

Three Times are good examples. In these tales the effendi appears as the symbol of a collective will rather than an isolated, happy-go-lucky, free-and-easy individual.

As a particular individual, Nasreddin is restless, some-times odd, but always anxious to know the world. He seeks to understand what happens around him and to express his *own* judgement on the events of life. He is self-assured, absolutely frank toward the rich and the powerful. It is a frankness sometimes heightened by an open and deliberate cruelty which is never accidental, irresponsible or boasting and defiant. These characteristics make Nasreddin a unique individual. He has to have his own say wherever he goes: at a funeral, at the bedside of a sick man, in the mosque or in the bazaar. His answers are always consistent with his personality. Because of this, the tales of the effendi possess an internal coherency.

From what has been said above, it is possible to con-clude that the diffusion of the Afanti tales in socialist China is not a casual accident. It is a fact which has to be seen within the framework of cultural strategy chosen by the Chinese. It is a strategy that aims to create a new culture which responds to the needs of the millions of people who have become masters of their destiny.

In reading the Nasreddin stories, therefore, one must try to break out of the restrictive framework of our own traditional methods of analysis. This means, first of all, trying to look at the stories not with an outside eye but, if possible, with Chinese eyes. The ideological content of the Nasreddin stories can be used in the work of ideological education today, as China moves forward to create a new and modern society and a new people.

A final note. Although we have translated these stories from the Chinese, a pure and simple translation was not sufficient. We also worked in our own way. We rewrote the text where linguistic differences obscured the humor and retouched expressions and dialogue when the two worlds and cultures ran the risk of not understanding each other. We have tried to reduce our intervention to the indispensable and have respected to the maximum the tone of the language. We have also worked to preserve the originality, that "difference" which is born of the very fact that the stories belong to another tradition. At the same time, we have sought to avoid the trap of an easier, more literal translation which would have resulted in a dubious exotism.

Primerose Gigliesi

Beijing
August 1981

THE PADISHAH'S CLOAK

Once the padishah gave a grand dinner, his guests being all rich and powerful people. During the banquet, the padishah presented each of them a splendid cloak. When he came to the Effendi Nasreddin, in front of everyone he gave him his donkey's saddle blanket of hemp.

The effendi took the saddle blanket from the sovereign's hands, bowed three times, then turned

to everyone present and said, "My lords, the cloaks that the padishah has given each of you are made of silk and satin, but they were only bought in the bazaar. Look at my gift — the padishah has given his very own cloak to me!"

THE GOOSE WITH ONE LEG

One day the Effendi Nasreddin went to give the padishah a fine goose already cooked. On his way he became hungry. He sat down on the sidewalk, opened the package and ate a leg.

When he arrived at the palace, Nasreddin, with great respect, made a beautiful bow and offered his gift. The padishah took it, looked it over carefully, then said, "Nasreddin, how is it that your goose has only one leg?"

The effendi didn't expect the padishah to look a gift goose in the teeth, so to speak, and at first did not know what to answer. But just then he saw a flock of geese out in the courtyard resting in the sun, each with one leg tucked up beneath it and balancing on the other. He hurriedly pointed them out to the padishah and explained, "But, Shadow of Allah, every goose in the world has only one leg, none of them have two. Look out in your courtyard."

The padishah at first widened his eyes. But then he ordered one of his guards to take a stick and

2

chase them. The poor fowls promptly unfolded their
legs and scattered in panic. The padishah smiled
coldly and said in a threatening tone, "Nasreddin,
tell me, which one of those geese has only one leg?"

"Padishah," the effendi answered without
blinking an eye, "they only look like they have two
legs because they run so fast. You have two legs,
but if somebody chased you that way with a stick,
you yourself would look like you had four!"

DEMOLITION

Once the Effendi Nasreddin went to see a rich lord and asked to borrow one hundred gold coins. When he got back home with the money, he and his family set to work and in two months built a two-story house. Admiring the new house, the lord thought he would take the second floor for himself in payment for the debt. So he went to find the effendi. First he spoke about the debt, then he asked for the apartment, and he threatened the effendi if he did not agree.

"All right," said the effendi. "You don't know it, but I was very worried that I might not be able to pay. It's an excellent solution, you take a big load off my shoulders."

So the lord and his family moved into the second floor of the new house. A few days later, the effendi called some of his neighbors together and with their help began tearing down the first floor. Hearing the racket downstairs, the lord ran to look out of the window. "Nasreddin, you're demolishing the house! Are you crazy?" he yelled in terror.

"Don't worry, go back inside! This has nothing to do with you." The effendi went on working.

"Nothing to do with me, nothing to do with me? I have something to do with it for sure!" He was trembling. "I am here on the second floor. If the house falls down, what will happen to me?"

"How can anything happen to you?" answered

the effendi. "We're tearing down the first floor, not the second! Just don't lean so far out of the window so you fall on our heads while we're working!" And he resumed systematically demolishing the first floor.

At his wit's end, the lord begged the effendi to listen to him. "Dear Nasreddin, in the name of our friendship, I beg you, please sell me the first floor."

"Sell? Oh no! Or ... well ... all right, give me two hundred gold coins."

"What? What?" the lord was speechless.

"Not one coin less, otherwise I demolish everything." And the effendi struck another blow with his sledgehammer.

"All right, all right!" shouted the lord, and hurried to get out his money.

THE DEVIL

At the bazaar, a broker said to the effendi, "I heard that you are on good terms with the devil, Nasreddin. Tell me, what does he look like?"

"Certainly," answered the effendi. "Look at yourself in the mirror."

THE CUP AND THE SAW

Once the effendi was a guest in the house of a rich and miserly lord. The lord filled his own cup to the brim with goat's milk and filled the effendi's cup only half way. "Drink," he said. "I have nothing good to offer you except this cup of milk."

"Sir," the effendi answered courteously, "could you first give me a saw?"

"A saw? What for?" said the lord in astonishment.

"Well, look . . ." and the effendi handed his half-filled cup to the lord. "The top half is useless, don't you think so? If we sawed it off, it wouldn't be wasted."

TOO QUICK A COUNT

There was a time in which the effendi lived as a lord, and everyone tried hard to become part of his circle of friends. One day somebody told him, "Nasreddin, what a great number of friends you have! How can you count them all?"

Shaking his head, the effendi said, "Count them? Well, for the moment, that's impossible. Later when I don't have a cent will be the time to count them."

THE FLYING HORSE

The padishah and the effendi went hunting together. The sovereign and his guards were mounted on splendid beasts, while the effendi followed them with difficulty on the old, broken-down horse the padishah had given him. When they reached the Gobi Desert a few hours later, a terrible wind came up and then rain began to pour. The padishah and his guards turned and galloped back to the city, reaching it so soaked that it looked as though they had fallen into a river.

The poor broken-down horse of the effendi, hearing the thunder, stopped and would not move farther. Seeing that things were turning bad, the effendi dismounted, took off his clothes and put them under the saddle. When it stopped raining, he dressed again and calmly ambled back to the city as if nothing had happened.

When the astonished padishah saw him coming with his clothes completely dry, he exclaimed, "How is it that you're not wet? Where did you go during the rain?"

The effendi bowed and answered, "I will tell you. But first, allow me to thank you: the horse you gave me was a flying horse. When you ran away, it was pouring. Then my horse soared into the sky and carried me to a beautiful garden. I had a very good time. But then I was afraid you would worry about me and I came back."

The padishah listened to him, very envious of

his good luck. So the next day he again invited the effendi to go hunting. But this time, as if by accident, he chose the old, broken-down horse for himself and left the effendi his own fine steed.

They galloped for quite a while and came again to the Gobi Desert. The hunting had just begun when, exactly as the day before, the wind began and the rain poured down. The effendi whipped his horse and in no time arrived at the walls of the city still dry. The broken-down horse, hearing the thunder, stopped and would not move farther. The padishah used the whip, hit him with his fists and kicked him, but the beast would not budge. The rain poured down heavier and the padishah went to bed that night with a good cold.

THE SHEEP AND THE WOLF

Once a big official saved a sheep from the jaws of a wolf. The sheep was then obliged to follow his savior home. But as soon as they arrived, the man decided to slaughter it. The poor beast began baaing with all its energy. The uproar was too much for

the effendi, who lived next door, and he came over to see what was wrong.

"You see this sheep?" the lord said. "I saved it from a wolf!"

"Then why is it cursing you?" asked the effendi.

"Cursing me?"

"Yes, he says that you too are a wolf."

THE MODEL DONKEY

Once, discussing officials with some people in town, the effendi commented sarcastically, "My friends, I tell you that even my donkey is more intelligent than the prime minister."

Soon enough these words reached the ears of the prime minister. He sent his soldiers to arrest the effendi and drag him before the padishah. There he accused him of outrageous slander and demanded that he be punished severely.

Angrily the padishah said to the effendi, "You stated that my prime minister is not as intelligent as your donkey. Do you have proof? If not, I will have your head cut off!"

"Of course I have proof," answered the effendi. "Once, while I was crossing a wooden bridge on my donkey, one of the animal's feet got stuck in a hole. The donkey, after some effort, succeeded in pulling his foot out. Not long after that, I happened to cross the same bridge, and you know what? — this fine animal was very careful not to step into that hole

again! But look at your prime minister: the people call him a thief from morning to night and still he doesn't stop robbing them. Your majesty, isn't my donkey more intelligent?"

"Hm-m-m, that's true," said the padishah slowly. Turning to the prime minister, he said, "Nasreddin is right. From now on, follow the example of his donkey."

13

THE WORTH OF THE PADISHAH

Once the padishah and the effendi were taking a bath together. Admiring himself, the padishah said, "Nasreddin, take a look, my physique's not bad, eh? If you had to sell me in the bazaar as a slave, how much do you think you could get?"

"Ten coins, at most," the effendi answered promptly.

"Idiot!" the padishah burst out in a fury. Picking up his silk scarf, he said, "Why, this alone is worth ten coins!"

"That's right," said the effendi, looking at the material carefully. "When I said ten coins, I was thinking of the scarf."

THE OFFICIAL AND THE BOAT

A high official had to cross a river together with the effendi. It was the first time in his life he had been in a boat. When they reached the middle of the river, the current became violent and the official turned green around the gills. Desperately he grabbed the effendi's arm and began to whine and plead for help: "Nasreddin, my dear Nasreddin, I have the feeling that I am about to give up my soul! Quick, find some way to make me not afraid!"

"Way?" said the effendi. "Ah, I have it . . . but maybe you won't like it."

"I'll like it, I'll like it, Nasreddin! Speak, please!"

"All right then. First of all you get into the water!" And the effendi picked up the official and threw him into the river. The functionary went down, came up, then went down and came up again. This happened several times. Then the effendi grabbed him by the hair and pulled him out.

When he was back in the boat, the official seemed much calmer. "Feel better now?" asked the effendi.

"Much better! I'm all right now," said the official.

"Eh," mused the effendi, nodding his head, "that's the way it is. Those who have never travelled on foot cannot appreciate a horse. Those who have never fallen into the water cannot appreciate a boat. The official who eats delicacies of every kind cannot appreciate hunger."

This time the official turned red, not green, and stalked off in silence.

WOLVES THAT DO NOT EAT SHEEP

One day an old shepherd said to the effendi, "Nasreddin, I have raised many sheep in my life, but sooner or later most of them were eaten by wolves. According to you, are there any wolves in this world that do not eat sheep?"

"Certainly," replied the effendi.

"Which ones? Tell me quickly!"

"The dead ones," answered the effendi.

THE GOLDEN RING

The effendi knew a rich merchant who had to travel into very far countries. One day before leaving on a trip, the merchant came to say goodbye to the effendi. Seeing that the effendi wore a golden ring, his eyes shone with envy. "My dear Nasreddin," said the merchant, "we are old friends and if we stay too long apart, I will feel very alone. This time I am going far away and who knows when I will be able to come back? What you can do is to give me your golden ring. When I look at the ring it will be as though I see you and I will have the impression that you are still next to me. . . ."

"Thank you, my friend. Your words move me," said the effendi. "Also for me this separation will be very hard. During your absence, I will think of you a lot. But the ring, *I* will continue to wear it. When I look at it, I will remember that you asked for it and that I didn't give it to you. It will be as though I see you and I will have the impression that you are still next to me."

MONEY AND JUSTICE

Once the padishah said, "Nasreddin, if you had to choose between money and justice, which would you choose?"

"Money," answered the effendi.

"What?" exclaimed the padishah. "I would choose justice. Money, after all, is not so rare. Justice, on the other hand, is very rare in this world."

"Men always desire what they do not have," replied the effendi. "In fact, you only want what you have never had."

THE SOUL OF THE PADISHAH

Talking with the effendi one day, the padishah asked him this question: "Nasreddin, listen: when I die will my soul go to heaven or hell?"

"To hell for sure," replied the effendi. "I have finally reached this conclusion."

The padishah lost his temper. His eyes flashed and he began a torrent of insults.

"But, Shadow of Allah, don't get so excited!" interrupted the effendi, trying to calm him down. "It is the only conclusion possible because you have killed so many people who deserved to go to heaven that the place is now too crowded to leave any room for you."

THE GOLD PLANT

The effendi borrowed a few grams of gold, then went out of the city one morning on the back of his donkey. When he reached the desert he got down, dug a hole and began dropping the gold into it. Just then, the padishah, as usual, passed by on his way hunting. Seeing the effendi at this curious task, he said in astonishment, "Nasreddin, what the devil are you doing?"

"Oh, your majesty, it's you. As you can see, I am planting a little gold."

Even more astonished, the padishah asked, "And after you have planted it, what will happen?"

"Oh, nothing unusual," answered the effendi. "Now I plant. On the fifth day I will come for the harvest, which will be about two pounds, and then I will go back home."

The eyes of the padishah shone with greed. Such a little investment, he thought to himself, even less than it takes to buy a fat tail of mutton. Then, with a great smile, he said, "My dear Nasreddin, planting such a modest quantity of gold won't make you rich. You should plant a little more. If what you have is not enough, come to the palace to get some more. I will give you as much as you want. We will consider it as though we had planted together. When the gold grows up, you will give me only eighty per cent of the harvest and keep all the rest."

"All right, your majesty."

The next day the effendi went to the palace of the padishah and got two pounds of gold. Two weeks later he brought the padishah more than ten pounds. The padishah opened his mouth in astonishment and, looking at the glittering metal, he got such pleasure that he couldn't shut it again. Then he ordered the guards to give the effendi all the chests in the treasury.

The effendi took the gold back home and distributed it to the poor. One week later, with empty hands, a frown and a sad expression, he went to the padishah. When the sovereign saw that sad face, he grew pale with anger. Narrowing his eyes into slits, he asked, "Ah, you are back? And the ox-carts with the gold in sacks, they are also here?"

"Your majesty, what a catastrophe!" The effendi began to weep. "You have seen yourself: it hasn't rained a drop for days. So the gold dried up! All of it was lost! Not only the harvest but even what I planted!"

Foaming with rage, the padishah came down

from the throne and began to swear. "Nonsense! Liar! Dried-up gold! Who do you think you're fooling?"

"All right, it seems strange to you," said the effendi, "but if you can't believe that gold can dry up, how can you believe that it can grow?"

The padishah subsided as though someone had stuffed a gag in his mouth.

THE OFFICIAL AND INTELLIGENCE

A new official arrived in the village and, of course, there was someone quick to praise him in front of the effendi. "The new official has a fine knowledge of the classics. He's a man with a fine brain, a head full of intelligence."

"Possibly," commented the effendi. "An official doesn't use intelligence, so of course it stays inside his head."

THE END OF THE WORLD

Some imams got together and agreed to play a joke on the effendi and eat his sheep. So they went to his house and began wailing, "Alas, poor us! Tomorrow is Judgement Day, the end of the world! Oh what a calamity!" Wringing their hands, they said, "Nasreddin, the sheep you have raised with so much patience must not be wasted. We are here to help you eat it." Having said this, they rushed to the sheep and cut its throat.

"Please," said the effendi. "If the end of the world is upon us, I agree. What point is there in keeping my sheep? Now calm down, take off your coats and go sit at the end of the garden where it's nice and cool while I cook the meat." The imams,

smiling contentedly, took off their coats and went to sit down in the garden.

Left by himself, the effendi built a wood fire, put the pan on and began to prepare the meal. He put the meat on to cook, then took the imams' coats, piled them on the fire and carefully burned them all. When the imams came back to eat and saw their coats reduced to a pile of ashes, they yelled, "Nasreddin, our coats!"

"What?" said the effendi. "Tomorrow is the end of the world and you want to keep your coats too!"

THE ROLLS AND THE PADISHAH

One winter, being without money for food, the effendi repaired his greenhouse and planted some melons. When they were ripe he chose the best of them and went to sell them to the padishah. Who could have imagined that the sovereign wouldn't pay a cent? The padishah complimented the effendi a great deal, declared that he was indeed a very good citizen and, with his mouth still full of melon, said, "Excellent! Excellent! Excellent!"

The effendi left the palace still hungry as a wolf, without one cent in his pocket. After a moment of reflection, he went into a restaurant, ordered twenty mutton rolls, sat down and ate them all. Then he got up and started toward the door, saying in a loud voice, "Excellent! Excellent! Excellent!"

"Hey, my money!" cried the restaurant keeper.

"What? I just paid you!" said the effendi, pretending to be astonished.

The restaurant keeper seized him and dragged

him before the padishah. Hearing that the effendi had eaten without paying, the padishah's face became dark. "So, Nasreddin, you eat and do not pay?"

"Your majesty, believe me, I haven't done anything wrong," answered the effendi. "This man is greedy, that's all. It's true I ate his rolls but I paid him with the three 'excellents' that you gave me — not even keeping one of them for myself."

The padishah shook his head in fury but couldn't say a word.

THE THREE TRUTHS

One day the effendi took his carrying pole and rope and went to the bazaar looking for work. He joined a group of day laborers waiting to be hired, squatted down and hoped for a bit of luck. After a while, a great lord came along and called out loudly, "I have bought a case of porcelain. To the one who will carry it home for me I will tell three incontrovertible truths."

No one paid any attention to him. The effendi, however, grew curious. "Money?" he thought. "There is always a way to earn it, but it doesn't happen every day to listen to three incontrovertible truths. If I carry the case for him I'll become more intelligent." He arose, picked up the case with his carrying pole and followed the lord toward his home.

As they walked, the effendi very humbly asked the lord to speak. The lord replied, "Listen carefully. If somebody tells you that it is better to have an empty stomach than a full one, you must absolutely not believe him."

"Wonderful!" exclaimed the effendi. "And what is the second truth?"

"If somebody tells you that to go on foot is better than to go on horseback, at any cost you must not believe him."

"Right! So right!" said the effendi. "It's such

a pleasure to listen to such profound truths! And what is the third truth?"

"Listen," said the rich lord. "If somebody tells you that in this world there is somebody more idiotic than you, for heaven's sake you must not believe him."

The effendi listened to him attentively, then suddenly opened the hand which was steadying his carrying pole and — crash! — the case burst open on the ground. Pointing to the broken pieces of porcelain, the effendi said to the lord, "Listen, if somebody tells you that your porcelain has not broken, for heaven's sake you must not believe him!"

THE INTELLIGENCE OF
THE FATHER

The padishah believed that he had a genius for a son. One day he asked the effendi to educate the young prince, thinking that if the effendi gave him lessons the boy would learn everything in a short while and become the most intelligent man in the empire.

A few weeks later, the effendi asked to see the padishah. "Your majesty," he said, "your son could study another ten years and it would be useless. I apologize for saying so, and I beg you not to be angry with me."

The padishah frowned with chagrin and annoyance, but later decided to send his son to study with the imam. One year later, the imam announced that the prince had finished his studies. The happy father gave a great banquet so that his son could demonstrate his intelligence.

When the party festivities had begun, the imam proudly proclaimed, "Our prince has finished his studies. Now he is the most intelligent person in the empire. He knows everything. For example, if you show him your fist and ask him what is in it, he can tell you in a flash. Would someone like to try?"

The effendi came forward from the crowd, hid something in his right hand, then approached the young man and asked, "What's in my hand?"

The prince looked at the effendi's hand for quite a while, then exclaimed jubilantly, "It's a flint!"

The effendi opened his hand and revealed a golden ring. With great admiration on his face, the effendi turned toward the crowd and said, "It's incredible! It's a miracle! The very same intelligence as his father!"

THE MONEY-SHITTING DONKEY

Once the Effendi Nasreddin rode his donkey to the palace of the padishah. Just before he reached the gate, he secretly pushed three gold coins into the donkey's anus. When he came before the padishah, the effendi announced, "My donkey doesn't shit turds but golden coins. Shadow of Allah, if you don't believe it, look!"

The astounded padishah opened his eyes wide and could not take them off the donkey's rear end. After a while, the donkey lifted its tail, pushed to relieve itself, and three golden coins fell on the floor.

"Then it's true!" shouted the padishah. "The money-shitting donkey really exists!" He was beside himself with excitement and immediately ordered wine, food and many dishes brought before the effendi. He even set the table himself. After the effendi had eaten and drunk his fill, the padishah

said, "My dear, dear Nasreddin, I pray you to sell me your donkey. I will pay you one hundred times more than it's worth."

"Your majesty, such a beautiful beast must, of course, belong to the padishah," said the effendi, bowing. "Give me the money and take the donkey." And the effendi went away.

The padishah, delirious with happiness, ordered a splendid velvet rug for the donkey to rest on. Then he called his favorite concubine, his son the prince, the nobles, the high officials and even the servants — in short, everyone in the palace — so they could see the wonderful money-shitting donkey. They waited a long time. Finally, the donkey began switching his tail. The sovereign jubilantly jumped down from his throne and shouted, "My golden coins! Quick, look! They're going to come out. . . ."

But when the donkey stopped moving its tail, there were only three ordinary turds steaming on the padishah's beautiful velvet rug.

THE DEBATE

The padishah believed himself a fountain of intelligence, and the thing that amused him most was to embarrass people with complicated questions. Once he had 12,000 scholars from all over the empire come to the palace and asked them where the center of the world was. Naturally, no one knew the answer. The padishah was jubilant. His satisfaction was so great that he had an edict proclaimed throughout the city promising a fortune to the one who could answer this question. The proclamation also added, "Whoever answers it wrong will be put to death."

A curious crowd gathered in the square, but after they heard the edict they all went away shaking their heads. The effendi, however, got on the back of his donkey and went to the palace of the padishah. He entered the courtyard, pulling his donkey, and asked to be received by the padishah.

"What?" exclaimed the padishah. "You know where the center of the world is?"

"Yes, your majesty," was the effendi's answer. "The center of the world is exactly under the hoof of the back left leg of my donkey."

"Imbecile!"

"If you do not believe it, you get the world and measure it. If I am wrong, you cut off my head."

"But . . . that's . . ." the padishah paused, then said, "Oh never mind. I'll ask you another question: How many stars are there in the sky?"

The effendi thought a bit and then answered, "First of all, it is necessary to state that there are neither many nor few. Then that there are exactly as many as the hairs in your beard."

"What nonsense!"

"It's right, your majesty, a hundred per cent right. If you do not believe it, you climb up in the sky and count them yourself. If there is even one less, I am ready to pay with my life."

"But . . . but . . . but then how many hairs are there in my beard? Quick, answer that!"

The effendi lifted the tail of his donkey with his right hand and at the same time pointed the index finger of his left hand at the chin of the padishah, then solemnly stated, "The hairs of your beard are exactly as many as the hairs in this tail."

The padishah banged his fist on the table and
yelled, "Wrong! Very wrong!"

"Your majesty, before you say whether it is
right or wrong, count the hairs of your beard first,
then count the hairs of my donkey's tail. . . ."

"Enough!" Suddenly, the padishah didn't have
the courage to say another word.

THE TALE OF THE EFFENDI'S BATH

The effendi was on his way to the public bath one day when he was surrounded by a bunch of street kids. "Tell us a story, Nasreddin! Tell us a story!" they chorused.

The effendi did not feel like stopping to tell a story, but no matter what he said the little hooligans would not leave him alone. Seeing that there was no way to escape, the effendi sat down on the ground and began.

"Once upon a time Nasreddin wanted to go to take a bath . . ." and with these words he stood up and started to leave. But the kids clutched him, saying, "More, more! Tell us more! So Nasreddin went to take a bath . . . and then what happened?"

"Bah! Who knows? You have kept him here, so how can I know what happened?"

THE WORST PLACE

Somebody once asked the effendi, "When one goes to a funeral, is it better to walk in front or behind the coffin?"

"In front or behind?" answered the effendi. "Both are all right."

The man asked him another question. "And according to you which is better, to be on the right or the left side of the coffin?"

The effendi beckoned the questioner close and whispered into his ear, "To tell you the truth, any place is good — in front, behind, right or left — so long as it is not inside."

A DINNER OF SMELLS

A poor man once went to find the effendi and humbly said, "Wise and noble Nasreddin, I want to ask a favor of you but I don't know if you will stoop so low as to help me."

"To help my neighbor is an honor and a pleasure. Speak," answered the effendi.

"Alas!" said the man with a sigh. "For us poor people, life is not easy. Yesterday I stopped a moment in front of the door of a restaurant belonging to a great lord. He said that I ate the smell of his food and asked me to pay him. Naturally I could not give him a cent and he took me before the cadi. My sentence will be pronounced today. Can you help me? Say something in my behalf."

"All right," replied the effendi and accompanied the poor man to the court of the cadi.

The lord was already there, talking gaily with the cadi. As soon as he saw the accused, the cadi changed his expression and began covering him with insults. "Shameless man! You see this lord? You have filled yourself up on the smell of his restaurant and have not even paid him. Pay him what you owe, at once!"

"You will become ill with vexation, my lord," said the effendi, stepping forward. He bowed and added, "This poor man is my elder brother. He doesn't have a cent, so I will pay in his place."

The effendi then took a little sack of copper

coins from his belt, bent to the lord's ear and jingled them. "Do you hear this sound?" he asked.

"Of course I hear it," retorted the lord.

"Well, now the debt is paid. My brother has smelled your meals and you have heard his money."

He took the arm of the poor man and went away.

THE THIRSTY POCKETS

Once the Effendi Nasreddin was invited to a dinner at the house of a friend. The host had prepared many delicate dishes: rice, mutton soup, jelly, pancakes, spiced-meat rolls and many, many varieties of fruit. When the time came to eat, the host told his guests not to stand on ceremony but to sit down and help themselves freely.

Sitting next to the effendi was a man who not only stuffed himself rapidly but filled his pockets with everything within reach. The effendi quietly picked up the teapot and began pouring tea into his neighbor's pocket.

"What are you doing? Are you crazy?" the man shouted in fury. "That's no kind of joke to make, particularly as a guest in the house of other people!"

"Excuse me, I have done nothing wrong," said the effendi. "Seeing that your pockets were so hungry, I thought they might be thirsty, too."

A STRANGE CARAVAN

One day the effendi was on his way to town to take care of some affairs. He had just passed the town gate when he saw the county magistrate, the cadi, the biggest landlord and the village head, busy gossiping in front of the mosque.

"What good wind brings you here?" one of them called out.

Pretending not to know them, the effendi answered, "I have something to do." And he went right on.

"Come join us a little bit," the others said. "Tell us something amusing."

"Excuse me, sirs, but I have no time," the effendi replied. "Just a few minutes ago, outside the town, I met a caravan. There were four camels, loaded with merchandise. The camel drivers said they were going to sell the merchandise to the county magistrate, the cadi, the landlord and the village head. So I must go to inform them that the caravan is coming."

The four men were instantly curious and said, "But do you know what they carry?"

"Yes, I asked them," answered the effendi. "The first camel is loaded with craftiness and the camel drivers said it was for the village head. The second camel was loaded with greed and they said it was for the landlord. The third was loaded with corruption and they explained that it was for the cadi. The fourth was loaded with tyranny and they have concluded that it is for the county magistrate because, of course, it couldn't belong to anybody else."

The four men did not understand. "Words, words! You speak and speak, but what kind of a caravan is that? And where are the four camels now?"

"It is a strange caravan," said the effendi, as though speaking to himself, "really strange. As for the four camels, at this moment they are right in front of me!" The effendi abandoned his questioners and went on toward the bazaar.

INVITATION TO LUNCH

There was once a man everyone knew as a lazybones. One day he met the effendi and said, "Nasreddin, tell your wife to prepare a good meal, I feel like eating at your place."

"Welcome," said the effendi politely, and set the time.

When the day arrived, the lazy man came very early to keep his appointment. "Here I am!" he exclaimed with a jolly face as he crossed the threshold. "Hurry, Nasreddin, bring some water so we can wash and begin to eat at once."

The effendi brought a water jar and, while he filled the basin, said, "Excuse me, but the lunch has not yet been served."

"What happened?"

"Everything is ready, but there is only one thing missing . . . just a little thing. . . ."

"What?"

The effendi brought his lips to his guest's ear and said, "The hands . . . the hands that do the work!"

THE GOVERNOR OF THE DONKEYS

The padishah wanted to humiliate the effendi. So one day he called him to the palace and, in front of all the ministers, he assumed a very solemn air and proclaimed, "Today I make a great announcement. I hereby confer on Nasreddin the title of governor of all the donkeys in the town!"

The ministers began to laugh. The effendi arose, made an elaborate bow, then with the greatest indifference passed in front of the padishah and went to sit on the canopy of the throne above the padishah.

"What impudence!" yelled the padishah. "How do you dare to sit higher than I? Come down from there at once!"

Most regally, the effendi raised his hands for calm. Then he said to the padishah and the ministers, "Whoa, there! Silence! A little respect! Am I or am I not your governor?!"

THE THING WHICH IS EATEN THREE TIMES

The effendi was walking on the street when he saw an old man huddled in a corner of the city wall all by himself. The man's head hung low and it was evident that he was in the midst of some serious worry. The effendi went up to him and said, "Brother, if there is something bothering you, speak freely and tell me."

The old man, seeing that the effendi was a poor man like himself, understood that he could pour it all out. "Alas," he said, "I am in a bad fix. The padishah put a copper coin in my hand and told me to buy something that could be eaten three times. He gave me three days and told me that if I do not find it he will have my head chopped off. I searched everywhere and couldn't find anything like that. Today is the third day and when the sun goes down behind those mountains it will be the end of me forever if I haven't accomplished the task!"

"Oh that's all. . . !" The effendi looked relieved. Taking the old man by the arm, he said, "Don't be afraid. The padishah won't chop your head off. Come with me."

He took the old man to the market where they bought a *hami** melon. Then together they went to the padishah.

---

* A melon native to Hami in Xinjiang (Sinkiang), so sweet that even the skin is eaten.

When the padishah saw the old man with the melon, he yelled to the executioner: "Come, come!"

"Your majesty, calm yourself," said the effendi, approaching the padishah. "My elder brother has satisfied your request. You see his melon? It is exactly what you are looking for. The first time you eat the flesh, the second the seeds and the third the skin."

The padishah looked dourly at the old man and let him go.

THE IMPERTINENT BARBER

The effendi had opened a barber shop. One morning the imam came in for a haircut. But when it was done he went away without paying. The effendi was so furious that he decided to get revenge.

A few weeks later, the imam came in again and sat down as if nothing had happened. The effendi quietly cut off all his hair. As he was shaving him he asked, "The eyebrows, you want them?"

"Certainly! Why do you even ask such a question?"

"All right, if you really want them, I'll give them to you. . . ." and with a couple of flicks of the razor the effendi eliminated the eyebrows of the imam and put them in his hand.

The imam almost suffocated with rage. But how could he argue? — he had said he wanted them.

"You want your beard also?" asked the effendi.

"No, no!" the imam said quickly.

"All right. If you don't want it, you don't want it. . . ." and with a few quick strokes of the razor the effendi eliminated the beard which lay strewn on the floor.

Panic-stricken, the imam looked at himself in the mirror — and saw a skull and face gleaming like an egg. This time he lost control of himself and, forgetting his manners, he began to swear.

"What? You even get angry?" retorted the effendi. "Didn't I do what you told me? If you had answered my questions properly, it wouldn't have happened! To tell the truth, I didn't feel like cutting your hair in the first place!"

THE OTHER FACE

One day the effendi played a practical joke on the padishah. The padishah took it badly and kicked him out of the palace, shouting, "Get out of here! I don't want ever to see your face again!"

A few days later, some illustrious scholars came from a neighboring country, presented themselves at the court with a difficult problem and asked the padishah to solve it. The padishah thought and twisted his brain, and for three days and three nights couldn't sleep or find the answer. Finally, one of his ministers said, "Your majesty, there is only one man on this earth who can answer this question — Nasreddin. Ask him to come to the palace and speak with these wise men."

Seeing no other way out, the padishah sent for Nasreddin. When the effendi entered the throne room, he turned at the door and walked backwards toward the padishah.

The padishah lost his temper. "What the devil

are you doing? Turn around at once and come here,
I need you!"

"How can I turn around?" asked the effendi
with great humility. "The last time you told me you
didn't want ever to see my face again, so the only
thing I can do is to show you my rear end."

MALE OR FEMALE

The padishah's favorite concubine was pregnant and he sent for the effendi to ask him if the child would be male or female.

"Female," was the answer.

"But what do you think, is a male or a female better?" asked the padishah.

"Male or female, it's the same — it's always a person," the effendi replied.

"Nonsense," exclaimed the padishah. "Women aren't worth anything. I want a male so that later on he will be able to take my place."

"Oh that's your problem, your majesty. Relax — if your place remains vacant, the people won't worry a bit."

A DOG FOR THE MAGISTRATE

The magistrate of the county asked the effendi to find a dog for him — one with a bad nature, ferocious and trained to bite people. A few days later the effendi brought him a calm, sweet-dispositioned dog that never barked even when a stranger came around. The magistrate, who had a bad temper, reacted violently. "Nasreddin, are you deaf? Didn't you hear what I told you?"

"Of course I heard," said the effendi. "The fact is that in your case any dog is all right. He only needs to stay with you a few days and he will not only learn to bite people but how to tear money chests apart!"

THE PREGNANT POT

Once the effendi borrowed a pot from a great lord. A few days later, the effendi put a smaller one inside and returned it. The lord was very satisfied because, after all, he was gaining something. Nevertheless, finding the fact rather odd, he

asked, "Nasreddin, how is it that inside my pot there is a smaller one?"

"Sir," said the effendi, "you probably didn't notice it but the pot you loaned me was pregnant. Two days later it gave birth to a little pot in my house. Therefore, today I brought back the mother and the baby."

"All right," said the lord, grabbing the mother and child. "From now on you can take all the pots you need so long as you give them back to me."

A few days later the effendi came back to the lord and told him that he had many guests and needed a very big pot. The lord, just waiting for such a thing, eagerly gave him the biggest and best one in his house.

A week went by. Another week. Then almost a month. But the effendi did not come back. The lord began to worry. Just as he was ready to go to the effendi's house, the effendi appeared, his eyes filled with tears. "Alas, my lord," he said, "two days later, your pot died in my house. At first I thought I would wait for the ritual forty days to pass before telling you. But I was afraid you could not wait anymore, so here I am."

"Nonsense!" cried the lord. "Don't think you can make jokes at my expense! The pot is iron, how can it die?"

"Sir," answered the effendi, "if a pot can give birth, it can surely die."

THE BEST DAY

The padishah said to the effendi, "You have crisscrossed the country on the back of your donkey and you are the only one who knows what the people think. So please answer this question: what has been, for my subjects, their best day?"

"Shadow of Allah, that day hasn't come yet," the effendi answered. "Your subjects' best day will be when you have the pleasure and supreme joy of going to Paradise!"

THE MOON AND THE WELL

One freezing night, though the padishah covered himself with forty blankets, he was still cold. Then he called the effendi to his side and said, "Nasreddin, if you are able to spend this night in the courtyard with only your shirt on, I will give you one hundred gold coins!"

"All right," answered the effendi and gave his padded coat to the padishah.

Out in the courtyard, the north wind was blowing so strongly it cut his face. Freezing to death, the effendi looked around and saw a stone mill at the foot of the wall. He began to push the enormous stone around, one turn after another, faster and faster. When dawn came, he was dripping with sweat

The padishah got up with the first rays of daylight, already enjoying the prospect of seeing the effendi stiff and dead. So his astonishment was great when he opened the window and saw Nasreddin in great spirits, running around and around the mill in circles. The padishah, who hated to part with one hundred gold coins, called out, "Was there a moon last night?"

"Yes."

"Then our bargain is off," said the padishah triumphantly. "If there was a moon, it was warm, in which case even I could have spent the night outside!" he added sarcastically. Seeing the padishah's ugly mood, the effendi decided it would be better to slip away quietly.

A few months later, the padishah and his ministers went hunting. It was full summer and at the edge of the desert it seemed like a furnace. The padishah and the ministers, dying of thirst, turned toward the effendi's house in the hope of getting some water.

The effendi was sitting on the wall of his well when he heard the imperious voice of the padishah: "Nasreddin, some fresh water! Be quick and serve us!"

"Please, please, make yourself at home," said the effendi.

"Where's the water?" scowled the padishah.

"Right here, your majesty, you see?" and the effendi stood on the wall of the well, leaning forward to look down inside.

"You only show me the water but don't give me a drink?" fumed the astonished padishah.

"Shadow of Allah," said the effendi, "if the rays of the moon can warm a person, the sight of water can extinguish his thirst."

A USELESS PRECAUTION

Once the effendi was passing the gate of the padishah's palace when he saw a small crowd working there. Curious, he approached and discovered that they were making the walls of the palace higher. The effendi, as usual, felt it his duty to ex-

press his opinion. "But the walls were high enough before. What is the point of building them higher?"

"You are dim-witted, Nasreddin!" said the ministers. "The point of building them higher is to protect the palace from thieves. They might climb over the walls and steal all the treasure of the empire!"

"Oh," said the effendi. Then, staring a long time at the ministers and advisors, he said, "Thieves won't be able to climb over the wall from the outside, but how can it protect from the thieves who are already inside?"

THE DEAD MAN

The magistrate of the county was gravely ill, asked many illustrious doctors to attend him and took many expensive medicines. In spite of this, he continued to be ill and it looked as though there was no remedy. Someone then thought of calling the effendi, who had cured many people.

The effendi arrived and, seeing the magistrate lying on the bed, turned toward the members of the family and said in an annoyed tone, "Doctors can only cure living people and you ask me to cure a dead man!"

In consternation, the members of the magistrate's family exclaimed, "But don't you see that the magistrate is alive?"

"True, at first sight he doesn't look dead," answered the effendi. "But the people say that the magistrate has no heart. Now tell me, how can he be alive?"

THE BEST WAY INTO PARADISE

The padishah asked the effendi to find a system for him whereby he could correct his own behavior and thus be able to enter Paradise.

The effendi said, "The best system is to sleep night and day, that is to say, not do anything."

"Nasreddin, are you serious? I can't believe that . . ."

"I assure you it's the best way to get into Paradise, your majesty," answered the effendi. "If you sleep, you cannot do more evil things. . . ."

A PROBLEM OF MEMORY

Once a man who had heard that the effendi was very wise began a long journey, walking many leagues to see him. At last, when he reached the effendi, he said, "I beg you to answer a question which has tormented me for a long time: what are the things in life to remember and what are the things to forget?"

The effendi thought a while, then answered. "If someone does something for you, remember it always. If you do something for someone, forget it immediately."

THE CLOTHES OF THE GUEST

Once the Effendi Nasreddin put on an old wornout robe and in such a state went to a banquet given by a friend. The friend, afraid that his guests would say that he associated with rags-and-patches people and that he would lose face, took the effendi aside and demanded that he leave.

The effendi went back home again, undressed in a hurry, put on a brand new robe and returned to the banquet. His friend looked at him from head to toe. Such luxury and elegance at once changed his attitude and with great affability he asked him

to sit down. Pointing to the many fine dishes, he said, "My dear friend, please serve yourself, please help yourself to whatever you want."

The effendi stretched out his arm toward the dishes and said to his sleeve, "My dear robe, please serve yourself, please help yourself to whatever you want."

Irritated, the master of the house exclaimed, "Nasreddin, what are you doing?"

"I am telling your noble friend, my robe, not to stand on ceremony."

THE BEST SOUND

Once a friend invited the effendi to lunch. This friend was very fond of music. Therefore, he showed the effendi all the musical instruments he had and played a piece of music on each one.

At noon the effendi began to be hungry. But the friend went right on playing. "Nasreddin," he suddenly asked, "according to you, which sound is best, the lute or the zither?"

"My dear friend," the effendi answered, "to tell the truth, right now I think there is no more beautiful sound in the world than that of a spoon scraping the bottom of a soup bowl."

THE CRAFTY ONE

The Effendi Nasreddin was sitting in front of his door writing to a friend when one of those good-

for-nothing people who do nothing all day long stopped behind him and began to read the letter over his shoulder. Without blinking an eye, the effendi went on, writing these words: ". . . I would like to tell you more things but now there is a bore so ill-mannered and brazen that he stands behind me secretly reading my letter and . . ."

At this point the man lost his temper and, coming around in front of the effendi with his arms akimbo, said, "Why do you insult me? Why do you say that I secretly read what you are writing?"

"You're a crafty one!" answered the effendi calmly. "If you haven't read anything, how do you know what I wrote?"

THE ADVICE OF ALLAH

The effendi was very poor and always hungry. One day he went to the bazaar. While he was wandering among the crowds he began to shout, "Sirs, listen! I am the Messenger of Allah!"

His voice attracted the guards, who immediately informed the magistrate of the county. The magistrate ordered the effendi brought to his house and said, "I have heard that you are a Messenger of the Almighty. Did Allah tell you anything that I should know?"

"Yes," answered the effendi in a solemn tone.

"But first bring me something to eat. One speaks better with a full stomach."

The magistrate, eager for Allah's message, ordered a meal served to him. The effendi ate slowly and when he was full he began like this: "Allah told me, 'Nasreddin, the magistrate has taken everything away from you poor people. Go to his house and eat as much as you can because that food also belongs to you.'"

THE DEATH OF THE PADISHAH

Once the effendi was joking with the prime minister and, among other things, he told him that he would die the next day. Who would have thought that the very next day the prime minister would lose his life in a fall from his horse? When the

padishah learned what had happened, he exploded with fury and sent his guards to arrest the effendi. "Nasreddin," said the padishah, "you have killed the prime minister! Choose your own punishment!"

"You are the one to say I am guilty," answered the effendi, "therefore, you must set the penalty."

"All right," said the padishah. "Then let's see. Since you can predict the fate of people so well, tell me when you yourself will die. But I warn you, if you do not know, this day will be the last of your life!"

"Of course I know. You must be joking," the effendi replied. "My death will take place two days before yours, that is to say, your majesty, forty-eight hours before you die."

The padishah paled. Fervently wishing that the effendi would live happily ever after, he let him go.

THE BAG OF TRICKS

The fame of the Effendi Nasreddin had gone beyond the borders of the nation. The padishah of a neighboring state, who had the habit of doubting everything, said to his ministers, "I have been told that not very far from here lives a man named Nasreddin who is able to trick even the padishah. Can such a thing be true?"

"Yes," his ministers replied. "We have heard

that Nasreddin is very intelligent and as far as cunning is concerned no one is a match for him, not even you, your majesty."

"Humph!" said his majesty. "I can't believe that! Think it over carefully: can a villain be craftier than a padishah?"

"Ah no," the ministers agreed with a convinced air. "It is not possible."

The sovereign decided to go into the neighboring state to become acquainted with this Nasreddin and play a trick on him which would prove that the brain of a padishah is always better than the brain of a man of the people.

He walked several days and finally arrived at the effendi's village. The effendi was working in the fields. The padishah, who was dressed as a pilgrim, asked him, "It is said that in this village there is a very astute man called Nasreddin. Can you tell him to come here? I would like to know just how justified his fame is."

The effendi, who had guessed the motive of this strange pilgrim's visit, said, "Nasreddin? I am he. How can I serve you?"

"Ah, so you are Nasreddin!" said the sovereign with a scornful smile. "I have heard that you are very cunning and that you have fun at the expense of everyone. I tell you that with me you will not win that game. No one has ever succeeded in fooling me."

"I want to try then," said the effendi. "But first you must wait for me a moment. I have to go home

and get my trick bag. If you are not afraid of my bag, lend me your horse so I can return at once."

"Even if you had ten trick bags, I wouldn't be afraid," said the padishah, handing the reins to the effendi. "Come back at once so I can test your talent."

The effendi climbed into the saddle and galloped off like the wind. The padishah waited until the sun was going down behind the mountain but no one came back. When he realized that he had been tricked he hid until it was dark and then began his journey back home.

THE TRIAL

The Effendi Nasreddin had offended the richest man in the town and the lord complained to the cadi and started a trial against him. Before he was taken to the cadi, the effendi got two stones and hid them under his shirt.

The cadi first asked him some questions. Then, while he turned the pages of the holy Koran with his knotted fingers, he secretly observed the attitudes of the two men. The effendi knew that, as usual, nothing good could be expected from the cadi. With a mysterious air, he touched his chest as though he were looking for something.

The cadi was sure now that the effendi had money for him, so he pronounced his verdict: "All right. According to the holy scripture and the law, Nasreddin is innocent." He lectured the rich man severely and ordered him to leave the court. Then, with a great smile from ear to ear, he said to the effendi, "So, you have won the trial. One really doesn't find a judge more just than I anywhere. Now give me what you have for me hidden under your shirt."

"At once," said the effendi, taking the stones out. Then, looking the cadi straight in the eye, he said, "If you had helped the other one, I would have bounced these two stones off your head!"

THE TRUNK AND THE THIEVES

One day three thieves entered the effendi's house. The effendi had seen them and hidden himself in a trunk.

The thieves searched everywhere for something of some value. At last, discouraged, they opened

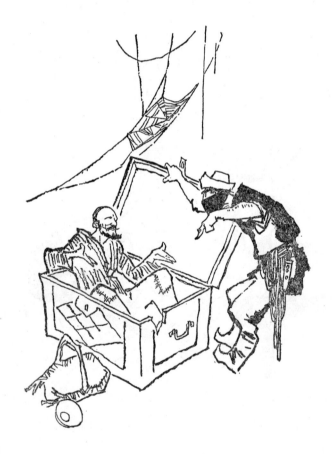

the trunk. "What are you doing here in the trunk?" exclaimed one of the astonished thieves.

"Excuse me," said the effendi politely. "Knowing that you couldn't find anything valuable in my house, I was so ashamed that I hid myself."

PAYMENT IN ADVANCE

Once the effendi went to a public bath house. The proprietor, thinking that he was a poor man, led him to a very dirty, decrepit bath and gave him a towel full of spots and holes.

When the time came to pay, the effendi put in the proprietor's money dish far more than all the other customers. A week later, he went again to take a bath. This time the owner bowed and scraped, led him to an impeccable private bath and put a brand new towel white as snow on the stool.

When the effendi was through washing, he went away without leaving a cent. "Sir!" cried the proprietor, running after him. "You forgot to pay."

"Not at all! Don't you remember? — the last time I was here I paid also for today."

THE SOURCE OF STRENGTH

The padishah wanted to know if there was anyone among the population stronger than he. So he sent for the effendi. "Nasreddin, you have travelled from one corner of the country to the other. Tell me, have you ever seen a man stronger than I?"

"Certainly, your majesty. Not one, but many," answered the effendi.

So proud of himself, the padishah was stunned. "And who are they?" he demanded.

"The men who work in the fields."

"Nonsense! What do the peasants do that is so extraordinary? Why are they stronger than I?"

"Shadow of Allah, be reasonable!" answered the effendi, annoyed. "The rice you eat, isn't it the peasants who give it to you? And if they didn't give it to you, where would you get *your* strength?"

EYEDROPS FOR A STOMACH ACHE

One day a man came running to the house of the effendi. As soon as he crossed the threshold, he began groaning, "I can't stand it anymore! Oh, my stomach! Please, Nasreddin, give me something for it at once!"

"How did it happen?" asked the effendi. "Did

you eat something hard to digest or something unclean?"

"I didn't eat anything . . . well, hardly anything. I only swallowed a big slice of spoiled cake. . . ."

"Ah," said the effendi and asked no more questions. He went to his little medicine chest and took out a bottle of medicine for the eyes.

"No, no!" exclaimed the man. "It's my stomach that hurts, not my eyes!"

"I've made no mistake," said the effendi. "If your eyes were not sick, how would you have eaten a spoiled cake?"

VISIT TO A PRISON

One day the padishah took the effendi with him on a visit to the prison. "What crime did you commit?" the padishah asked the prisoners.

"None!" yelled the men in unison.

The padishah began questioning each by turn and, it seemed, there was only one guilty person among them.

"Protector of the Universe," the effendi said to the padishah, "please order this man kicked out of here at once! How could he have gotten himself into this place? It is inadmissible that there are people like this in your prisons!"

THE MIRACLE

Once the effendi took a piece of white cloth, bandaged his eyes and pretended to have lost his sight. Then he went to the cadi. The cadi knew that the effendi had never been very devoted, so he seized this opportunity to give him a sermon. "Now you understand what it means not to believe in Allah? Isn't it He who has deprived you of sight? But Allah is compassionate. Quick, get down on your knees and pray for his forgiveness. He is the only one who can help you."

"All right," said the effendi. After he had prayed, he tore the bandage from his eyes and exclaimed, "Now take me to see Allah, the Compassionate! He has helped me and I want to thank Him."

The cadi, scared to death, retreated in panic, stuttering "I . . . I . . . really . . ."

THE SCHOLARLY TURBAN

The Effendi Nasreddin, who had wrapped a nice turban around his head, went out of his house for a walk. Suddenly, a man came toward him and, after looking at the effendi's head, said, "Master, please read this letter for me."

"I don't know how to read, I am illiterate," answered the effendi.

"Don't be so modest. With such a turban you surely must be well educated."

The effendi then took off his turban and put it on the man's head. "If education depends on the turban," he said, "I give it to you and you read the letter by yourself."

THE JOB THAT SPOILS THE SIGHT

The effendi had a friend in the village whom he had liked very much since they were children and from whom he would have liked never to separate. But many things happen in life. The friend was appointed as a high official and had to

live in the capital. Some time later, the effendi left the village to go and see him.

But now the friend was proud and arrogant. He pretended not to know the effendi and asked, "What is your name? To what do I owe the honor of your visit?"

The effendi became red as fire and began to yell, "What, you don't recognize me? I am Nasreddin and when we were young you were my best friend! Shame! — becoming an official has made you blind!"

GIFT

The imam went to visit the effendi, who ordered his wife to bring yogurt and biscuits at once. While they were eating and talking animatedly, the imam suddenly spoke of the effendi's house. "Nasreddin," he said, "you live in a dog's hovel! But don't be upset about it. Men do not remain long on this earth. Whatever adversities there are, it does not matter. In the other life, Allah will repay you with a beautiful house, double the size of this one and full of light. Do not worry."

"Venerable imam," said the effendi, "if Allah wants to give me a house, please tell him to give it to me now. When I pass into the other world, maybe I won't need one as big as he offers."

THE GLUTTON

There was a very rich and very idle lord. Once he thought he would make fun of the effendi. He bought a large number of melons and invited the effendi and many other people to a lunch. While the rich man urged his guests to eat, at the same time he kept slipping his own melon peels onto the effendi's dish. When the melons were finished, he pretended great surprise and exclaimed loudly, "But friends, look at the peels on Nasreddin's dish! What a glutton! He has eaten more than all of us together!"

"Ha ha ha!" laughed the guests.

"Ha ha ha!" laughed the effendi in return. "The glutton at this table is not me. At least I left the peels. But look at our host's dish — he has eaten everything, peels and all!"

ALLAH COLLECTS INTEREST

The effendi urgently needed money but could find no one who could lend him ten dinars. Not

knowing what he could do anymore, in the middle of the night he began to implore the All-Merciful: "Allah, All-Merciful, I pray, grant me this favor, give me ten dinars. If you cannot give them to me outright, I would be satisfied even with a loan."

The effendi had not finished his prayer when he heard somebody knocking loudly at the door. He signalled his wife to go to the door. The visitor was the local official governing one hundred families*. "Nasreddin," he began, "it is necessary again to repair the mosque. Allah, who protects you in every hour of the day, said that your part for the work is five dinars."

The effendi sighed and said, "Alas, Allah asks very high interest! He has not loaned me anything yet and already he wants to be paid back!"

INFALLIBLE TECHNIQUE

Someone was going around saying that the effendi was an excellent archer. The padishah became curious and invited him to go hunting with him. When they were half way, they saw a large tree some distance away. The padishah ordered the effendi to hit it with an arrow. The effendi loosed his first arrow without reaching the target. The padishah began to sneer.

---

* An administrative system organized on the basis of households.

"Don't laugh, your majesty," said the effendi, "this is your technique." Then he launched a second arrow. But even this time it did not reach the tree. The padishah sneered again.

"Don't laugh, your majesty," repeated the effendi, "this is the technique of your ministers."

Then he shot the third arrow straight into the center of the trunk of the tree. "That," said the effendi with a deep bow, "modestly speaking, is the technique of Nasreddin!"

THE CURSE

Walking on the street one day, the effendi suddenly was hit by a stone. Angrily pointing his finger at the stone, he cried, "I curse you one thousand times!"

By chance a master of the Koran passing by heard these words and thinking they were meant for him he went to the cadi to denounce him.

The cadi summoned the effendi and instead of questioning him, condemned him to pay a fine of

half a dinar. The effendi took out one dinar and threw it on the table. Turning toward the cadi, he declared, "You fined me half a dinar for one thousand curses. Here is one dinar. Now I curse you a thousand times. We are even!"

THE MUTTON BONE

There was an official who governed one thousand families. One day while he was eating a piece of mutton, a bone went down his throat crossways and he could neither spit it out or swallow it. He was in such a bad state that it looked as though he was going to die any moment. Many illustrious doctors were called but none of them succeeded in taking the mutton bone out of his throat. Then someone thought of calling the effendi.

The effendi, however, only gave the messenger a letter, saying that this letter would be the best medicine for the official.

When the sick man read the letter, he shouted once, rolled his eyes and fell back dead. The relatives and friends grabbed the letter. It read: "Illustrious Lord, you have committed thousands of crimes. Today you have eaten a piece of mutton and even this you stole from the poor people. The bone has choked you and it is just what you deserve! Now, die quickly, it is the best thing you can do!"

A BREATH OF AIR

One evening the effendi was crossing a graveyard when in the distance he saw some men approaching on horseback. Suspicious, he said to himself, "Ten to one, these people are bandits" and he hid in a tomb.

Unfortunately, the men on horseback had seen him. They rode up to the tomb and called out, "Who are you?"

The effendi stuck his head out. "I am a dead man."

"And what is a dead man doing out at this hour?"

"Breathing the fresh night air."

"Dead men don't need to breathe fresh air!"

"Ah, you are right," said the effendi. "I made a mistake." And he withdrew into the tomb again.

THE LAZY FELLOW AND THE DONKEY

In the town there lived a man who was extremely lazy, so lazy that he wouldn't even walk fast. One day he decided to go to the bazaar, so he went to the effendi's house to ask if he could borrow his donkey. The effendi answered, "My friend, if you walk a little faster you can get to the bazaar just by walking. Besides, my donkey is not here."

Just then, however, the donkey started to bray. The man's face brightened and with a big smile he said, "You hear that? Your donkey is telling me that he is here. . . ."

"I really pity you," the effendi said. "You are so lazy that you cannot even think. You do not believe a respected man with a beard such as mine and yet you accept what a donkey says!" And the effendi shut the door.

⑤

阿 凡 提 故 事 选

李丽玫　费蘭德　译

*

新世界出版社出版（北京）

中国国际书店发行

1982年　第一版

编号：（英）10223—113

00100

10—E—1645 P

To Maria, Ande, An[...], Santiago,

Thank you for everything ... next time I won't be so wimpy!

"Gently,"

Michele

XMAS 1984

Polly's Pointers

Polly's Pointers

1081 Helpful Household Hints for
Making Everything You Own Last Longer

Polly Fisher

Rawson, Wade Publishers, Inc. New York

Polly's Pointers is based on columns by Polly Cramer and Polly Fisher written for Newspaper Enterprise Association.

Library of Congress Cataloging in Publication Data

Fisher, Polly.
  Polly's pointers.

  Selections from the author's daily newspaper column.
  Includes index.
  1. Home economics. I. Title
TX158.C763   640   81-40272
ISBN 0-89256-184-X   AACR2
ISBN 0-89256-197-1 (pbk.)

Published simultaneously in Canada by McClelland and Stewart, Ltd.
Composition by American–Stratford Graphic Services, Inc. Brattleboro, Vermont
Printed and bound by R. R. Donnelly & Sons Co., Crawfordsville, Indiana

Designed by Jacques Chazaud

First Edition

Table of Contents

How to Use Use This Book

We've been called the throwaway society. Use it once and throw it away, right?

Wrong.

In these days of inflation, a depressed job market and high taxes, you can't afford not to make everything you own last as long as possible. That means being able to clean it, repair it, preserve it and reuse it.

No matter which of these household chores is facing you at this moment, there's a way you can do it more easily, more thoroughly, faster and cheaper. Over a million people throughout the country are learning how every day in our daily newspaper column "Polly's Pointers." Now, for all of you who are already old friends and for all of you who will become new friends, we've collected the best of the hundreds of thousands of pointers contributed by our readers and discovered through our own experience.

These suggestions, hints, tips and techniques will save you time, money and labor. You'll find ways to make use of things you used to throw away and ways to preserve your most treasured possessions. You'll learn how to do things simply without spending money on a closetful of specialized cleaning products and gadgets. We'll help you beat inflation without lowering your standard of living.

How to Use This Book

We've tried to organize this book simply and logically so that you can quickly find the information you need. In most cases, by using the table of contents and index, you can easily look up whatever problem you want to solve right now and find one or more ways to deal with it. Most of the chapters are *alphabetically arranged* to make finding information easier. We want you to spend your time trying out our pointers, *not* helplessly leafing through the book without finding what you need to know.

You'll find that many problems have more than one suggested solution. Pick the one that seems the most logical in your particular circumstances. Some solutions may use products you already have on hand, others may be indicated for particularly sensitive or delicate items, and some remedies are last-ditch, emergency measures when nothing else will do the job.

Always use common sense when selecting a remedy. Be sure to consider the type of material on which you're going to use a cleaning solution, and try to determine whether it is compatible with that solution. Always test a cleaning product in an inconspicuous spot if you're unsure about how it will react. Also be sure to work in a well-ventilated area when using any product that gives off potentially dangerous fumes. Handle flammable products, acids and poisonous substances with extreme care, using rubber gloves if necessary. Keep all such substances well out of the reach of children and pets.

We've divided this book into four sections. CLEAN IT will show you how to get a brighter, cleaner wash without having to buy every expensive laundry additive on the market; how to remove the most stubborn stains from your carpets, floors and clothes; how to banish household odors, rid your house of insect pests, and make your entire house sparkle. REPAIR IT will save you hundreds of dollars by showing you how to salvage clothing, repair furnishings and maintain the outside of your home without calling in professional help. In PRE-SERVE IT, you'll find simple tricks that can prevent future household chores—how to keep silver from tarnishing, for example, or how to store clothing to prevent fading, mildew and odors. We've also given you tips for proper food storage, creative ideas for using leftovers and rescue techniques for recipes that didn't turn out quite right. And you'll never throw away anything again before consulting REUSE IT, recycling pointers for ways to use plastic bags, cartons, bottles, old linens, clothing and many other items over and over again.

So now that we've given you some idea of what's in store for you, start today to save money with any one of the pointers in this book. You and your family will have happier, more carefree lives when you start making things last!

PART I

Clean It

CHAPTER 1

Laundry Blues (and Whites, and Yellows, and Pinks...)

Now that clothing prices are soaring out of sight, you know you've got to make what you have last as long as possible. Keeping your family's clothes fresh and new-looking starts with cleaning.

These pointers will help you get a cleaner, brighter wash without wasting money on every new miracle additive and detergent on the market. They'll explain how to treat stains on both washable and nonwashable fabrics. You'll find special care instructions for fibers like wool and silk, and materials like leather and vinyl. Above all, these hints can help you save money—by allowing you to cut down on professional dry cleaning, and because in most cases, these cleaning methods use common, inexpensive household products you already have in your cleaning closet or kitchen.

Please remember to follow these guidelines when trying out any pointer:

Always test any unfamiliar product or cleaning method on an inconspicuous place before treating an entire article. Some solutions work perfectly well on some fabrics and not on others. Some dyes are colorfast; others, on the same type of fabric, are not.

Use common sense when selecting a remedy, taking into account the fabric and your past experience with cleaning that particular garment. If a dress is labeled "dry clean only," and you're not sure if it will be damaged by water, don't use any water-based cleaning solution or regular soap or detergent. Use instead one of the "dry cleaning" methods involving a nonwater-based product. Of course, if you've tried everything and you're going to throw away a garment if you can't get it clean, you have nothing to lose by resorting to more drastic measures, but try it on a small and inconspicuous place first.

Whiter Whites

Here are some ways to whiten washable fabrics. When the dingies, the yellows, and that allover tattletale gray begin to get you down, try one of the following remedies:

Rinse and soak articles in cold water. Make up the following solution in a plastic bucket: 2 to 2½ gallons hot water, ½ cup liquid cholorine bleach and ½ cup automatic dishwasher detergent. Mix thoroughly, let cool and then place articles in this solution so they are completely submerged. Soak 3 or 4 hours and then wash as usual. Synthetic whites and white cottons will be much whiter and free of most stains.

Packaged color remover will frequently remove stains and dinginess when nothing else works. Just follow package directions. Color remover is available in the home dye section of variety stores and supermarkets.

Cream of tartar is excellent for restoring whiteness, especially for baby clothes and diapers on which you don't want to use harsh bleaches and chemicals. Add a teaspoon or two of cream of tartar to a gallon of hot water, then soak garments overnight. Great for linen handkerchiefs and delicate synthetic knits, too.

The gradual graying of white fabrics is frequently caused by inadequate rinsing. Try putting 1½ cups of chlorine bleach and ½ cup of detergent in the first washer cycle only (on most machines, this is called the soak or presoak cycle). Continue through the subsequent wash and rinse cycles using only clear water. You'll be sure all the soap is rinsed out for a brighter wash.

Old-fashioned bluing is effective, particularly on yellowed fabrics. It actually works by tinting fabric a very, very faint blue, which your eye perceives as white.

Hang your wash out in the sun to dry for a day. The bleaching effect of the sun is great for white fabrics, but use caution: the sun can fade colors as efficiently as it whitens whites.

For badly stained or yellowed fabrics, chlorine bleach is better than oxygen (all-fabric) bleach. Oxygen bleach only maintains whiteness; chlorine bleach restores whiteness.

Vinegar can brighten your laundry by breaking up soap buildup. Add ¼ to ½ cup white vinegar to the rinse cycle in your washing machine, a smaller amount to your basinful of hand laundry. Vinegar also softens fabrics. Any slight vinegar odor will disappear when the garment is dry.

Freezing can bleach white woollens safely. After washing and rinsing, put sweaters, scarves, etc. in the freezer for an hour or so, then allow to thaw normally and dry.

Some emergency measures: If your fabric is so delicate that bleaches, detergents and other chemicals might weaken the fibers, small spots and stains can be hidden by dabbing with white typewriter correction fluid. You'll have to reapply after laundering or dry cleaning.

When dingy bras, panties and slips will no longer become white no matter what you do, dye them in strong hot tea, then rinse in cold water. The result will be a delicate ecru color—a natural no-show color particularly nice under sheer blouses!

First Aid for Stains

Baby formula These are basically protein stains and should be laundered in an enzyme detergent. Stubborn formula stains can be rubbed with a paste of meat tenderizer and water, or the garments can be soaked in hot water to which you have added a teaspoon or so of cream of tarter.

To head off the problem of old set stains on baby's clothes, keep a closed diaper pail filled with cold water and about ¼ cup laundry presoak detergent. When you change the baby's clothes, simply drop them immediately into this pail and let them soak until you are ready to wash them. Keep another such pail just for diapers, but add some borax to whiten diapers and destroy odors.

Blood Soak fresh bloodstains in cold water, then sponge with warm suds and rinse. If such a stain persists, sponge with an ammonia water solution (about 3 tablespoons to each gallon of water).

A paste of starch and water left to dry often removes old bloodstains from heavy fabrics and mattresses.

Try wetting a blood spot with water, then shake on a little meat tenderizer. The enzyme in the tenderizer is supposed to break down the protein of the cell wall. Leave on fifteen to thirty minutes, then sponge with cool water and wash as usual.

You can also make a paste of the meat tenderizer and water and apply that to the fabric.

Hydrogen peroxide will also remove bloodstains. Sponge on, let it stand for a minute or two, then blot with a damp cloth. Stains that have been set for a while may require more than one application; simply repeat the procedure until the stain is gone. Launder as usual.

Chewing gum   Rub gum with ice to harden, scrape off excess and sponge remaining stain with dry-cleaning fluid. Lighter fluid may also work, but use extreme caution when working with any flammable chemicals like this.

Another suggested remedy to soften chewing gum on fabrics is to spread egg white over the gum, then launder.

Chocolate   Rub with warm water and mild soapsuds, then rub lightly with a commercial dry-cleaning fluid (available in supermarkets).

Coffee and tea   Coffee and tea stains should be treated with the boiling water treatment described for fruit stains. If the coffee has cream in it, the spot should then be treated as for grease stains.

An emergency treatment for food and beverage stains of many kinds, and one that is handy even while dining out, is ordinary club soda. Pour, sponge, dab or otherwise wet the fresh stain with club soda and blot up with a clean cloth, napkin, or even tissue.

Crayon Loosen crayon stains with kitchen shortening, such as Crisco, and then apply detergent. Work it into the stains until the outline is removed, then launder. If stains remain, pretreat before laundering with a liquid household cleaner.

Fruit stains Stretch stained area of fabric over a large bowl, fasten with a rubber band and pour boiling water through the stain. If hot water could damage your fabric, sponge with cool water. If stain still remains, sponge with hydrogen peroxide or a lemon juice and water solution.

Glycerine can also remove fruit stains. Work glycerine into the stain and let the fabric sit for several hours. Then add a few drops of white vinegar and rinse thoroughly before laundering.

Glue To remove mucilage, apply a detergent solution. If stains remain, use a white-vinegar solution (¼ cup white vinegar to ¾ cup warm water), let it stay on about fifteen minutes and then launder.

On household cement, apply nail-polish remover with an eye dropper, sponge with a clean cloth. Do not use this on synthetics.

To remove plastic model cement, immerse stain in a ten-percent white-vinegar solution, keep at the boiling point for fifteen minutes or so and then rinse.

To remove rubber cement, use a grease solvent.

Dried white glue can often be removed with household ammonia. Soak garment in warm water, then apply ammonia to the glue spots, rub between your fingers and rinse out with clear water. Rub dry with a cloth.

To remove sticky glue left by price tags and adhesive labels, sponge with rubbing alcohol or lighter fluid or soak spots in hot white vinegar.

Grease and tar   If spots are hard and dry, apply petroleum jelly, rub between the hands and then apply dry-cleaning fluid. If stain remains, work detergent into it, then launder.

Bar soap cleans grease off your hands and it can do the same for your clothes. Rub soap in well and rinse.

Waterless hand cleaner (available in drugstores and many hardware stores) will remove stains left by both grease and tar. Apply the cleaner to the stain, rub it in gently, then launder. Paper towels can be used under the stain to absorb the grease and excess cleaner while you're working it into the fabric.

A very safe remedy for grease stains is cornstarch. This is good for fabrics that shouldn't be touched with water and for napped fabrics like velvet or fur. Rub cornstarch into the spot, press with a warm steam iron (place a towel under the spot to absorb the grease), then brush away the excess cornstarch. Be sure to use a press cloth on top for wool or napped fabrics.

Instant first aid for grease stains is as simple as carrying a small bottle of talcum powder in your handbag. The next time you spill salad dressing or drip melted butter on your clothes while dining out at a fancy restaurant, sprinkle talcum powder on the spot, let it stand a few minutes and then brush off. No grease stains to mar your grand exit or spoil the rest of the evening!

Greasy collars and cuffs

Try using shampoo—one designed for oily hair if the stains are very bad—as a presoak solution. Rub the fabric to make a lather, let stand a few minutes, then wash as usual. A clean squeeze bottle is excellent for applying shampoo, detergent or an ammonia and water mixture to such stains. On very tough spots, ammonia and water rubbed in with a medium bristle brush is effective.

Ink

Ball-point pen ink can be removed with hair spray. Spray the ink stain thoroughly, let dry and then launder.

Fresh stains from pen inks of various kinds, carbon paper, and printing ink can frequently be removed with rubbing alcohol. Sponge on and rinse.

Try sponging ink stains with sour milk or a mixture of half milk and half vinegar. Repeat if necessary.

An inexpensive and handy solution for removing printer's ink stains is petroleum jelly. Place an old towel or stack of paper towels under the stained fabric, rub petroleum jelly into the stain and then flush out with a dry-cleaning fluid. Repeat until the ink stops "running." Wash as usual.

The U.S. Department of Agriculture recommends the following remedy for stains from printer's ink. Sponge such stains with turpentine or use a commercial grease solvent (sold under various trade names) as follows: place stained area stain side down on a pad of clean cloth and apply solvent with a light motion, "washing" it out onto the cloth. A wad of cottton or soft cloth is useful for applying the solvent. Use several light applications if necessary. Work from center of stain out and irregularly around the edges so as to prevent rings. Change pad underneath if necessary.

India ink stains are almost impossible to remove if they are allowed to dry, but you might try this procedure. Remove all pigment from a fresh stain so that it will not spread. Wash with detergent and let stain soak in warm suds to which you have added 1 to 4 tablespoons ammonia for each quart of water (use the greater quantity of ammonia for older, heavier stains). Dried stains may have to be soaked in this solution overnight.

Fresh iodine stains usually wash out easily. For older stains, **Iodine** sponge with alcohol or a solution of a few drops of ammonia in ½ cup of water. Soak if necessary. When stain has disappeared, wash in warm suds and rinse at least twice.

To remove a make-up ring from the neck of a blouse with- **Make-up** out having to launder the entire blouse, dip a toothbrush in a mixture of baking soda and water and brush the ring very lightly. Rinse by brushing with clear water and blot dry with a towel. Good for delicate fabrics.

Lipstick stains can be softened with glycerine, then laundered in as hot water as the fabric will stand.

On nonwashable garments, lay the lipstick-stained fabric face down on paper towels, sponge the back with a dry-cleaning solvent and replace the towels with clean ones to absorb the red color. When the stain has disappeared, dampen the spots with water, rub with bar soap, and rinse with cool water.

Toothpaste will also frequently remove lipstick stains. Rub onto the stained area, then wash as usual.

Perfume stains and stains made by alcoholic beverages can be treated with rubbing alcohol. Just sponge it on. Dilute alcohol with two parts water for use on acetate fabrics.

Fingernail-polish spots should be sponged with pure amyl acetate (available at drugstores), then laundered. If stain persists, sponge with rubbing alcohol to which you have added a few drops of ammonia. Do not use nail-polish remover on fabrics.

Mildew and rust stains

Light mildew or rust stains on white fabrics can be rubbed with lemon juice and salt, bleached in the sun for several hours, then washed in sudsy water and rinsed. Buttermilk is also effective on mildew stains. Soak as long as it takes the buttermilk to bleach out the stain, anywhere from one to twenty-four hours depending on the severity of the stain.

Older, heavier mildew stains are difficult to remove, but hydrogen peroxide may work on such spots. Sponge on the peroxide, then launder with a bleach that is safe for the fabric in question. Remaining stains on less delicate fabrics can be soaked in bleach water (1 tablespoon bleach to a quart of water) for fifteen to twenty minutes, rinse and wash.

As a last resort for tough rust stains, try oxalic acid (available from your druggist, but use with caution: this substance is poison). Dissolve 1 teaspoon oxalic acid in a cup of barely warm water and pour back and forth through the spot. A small spot may be dipped up and down in the solution. When stain has been removed, rinse immediately.

Mud

Let fresh mud stains dry completely, then brush well. If this does not remove the stains from nonwashable but colorfast garments, sponge with cool water by forcing the water through the stain. If it still remains, rub detergent on and work it into the fabric. Rinse. A final sponging with alcohol helps remove all the detergent and the fabric will dry more quickly. Dilute the alcohol with 2 parts water before using on acetates.

Paint

Turpentine should remove most oil paint stains. Sponge on until paint softens, scrape off any excess, rinse and launder as usual.

Mechanics' waterless or cream hand cleaner is good for oil or acrylic paint spots. Rub in and let it rest—the older and harder the spot, the longer you should let the cleaner work before washing.

Baby oil will also remove many types of paint spots. It's especially effective in cleaning paint (oil, acrylic or latex) from your hands and fingernails.

When latex paint has dried, it is extremely difficult to remove. Fresh, wet spots can be washed out in warm water and soap. For dried latex paint spots, try saturating the stain with rubbing alcohol.

Varnish stains should be rubbed with petroleum jelly, then soaked in turpentine. While soaking, rub the stains occasionally until they soften and can be rubbed off, then wash and rinse.

Pencil

Rub a thick detergent and water paste into pencil marks with a finger, then add a few drops of ammonia and rub it in. As the stains dissolve, rinse them away with warm water.

Perspiration and deodorant

Sponge old stains with white vinegar and new ones with ammonia. Rinse and launder in as hot water as fabric permits. For very stiff stains, soak the area in warm white vinegar, then rinse and launder.

To remove strong odors frequently left by such stains, see the section on "Laundry Odors," page 109.

Plastic, melted

To remove hardened plastic melted onto fabric, place stain side down on several layers of paper toweling, cover with another layer of toweling and press with a hot iron. As plastic melts off the fabric onto the paper, replace the towels with fresh ones. Repeat until all plastic has melted onto the towels. If the plastic spot is very heavy, the heat may soften it enough so that the bulk of the plastic can be scraped away with a dull knife.

Scorch

Heavy scorch marks cannot be removed. However, if the fibers are stained but not really burned, dampen a cloth with hydrogen peroxide, lay on the scorched spot, cover with another pressing cloth and iron over it with your iron set on the hottest setting safe for your particular type of fabric. Rinse with clear water.

To remove shiny spots from a variety of fabrics, sponge **Shine** with hot vinegar or an ammonia solution of 1 tablespoon per quart of water. Cover with a damp cloth and press with a warm iron on the right side. Brush when dry if needed. Certain wools look better after a light brushing with fine sandpaper to make the fibers perk up.

This is a common problem on draperies. To make water **Water spots** spots disappear, add enough vinegar to several tablespoons of baking soda to make thick paste, spread the paste on the stains. Allow to dry, then wash in sudsy water or dry-clean as appropriate.

To remove candle wax, first scrape off any blobs of wax **Wax** with a dull knife. Then place stained area between several layers of paper toweling and press over the top toweling with a hot iron. This will dissolve the wax and transfer it from the cloth to the absorbent paper. Keep shifting or changing the toweling as the wax is absorbed into it.

When colored candles leave spots on colored fabrics, soak stains in 1 part alcohol and 2 parts water (do not use alcohol on acetates). Then wash and rinse. Diluted bleach will remove colored wax stains from white fabrics.

Wine stains can be treated in the same manner as fruit **Wine** stains. Or, they can be soaked in buttermilk before laundering.

Special Fabrics

Feather pillows

Yes, feather pillows as well as synthetic pillows *can* be washed. Pillow ticking is so thick that sudsy water will not get through to the feathers, so rip open about five inches of the seam of each short end. Sew these openings with big loose stitches and heavy thread to keep the stuffing from falling out.

Two average-sized pillows are about right for most home machines. If you're washing only one, add a couple of towels to balance the load. Use a bit more soap or detergent than for a regular washload, as the pillows hold a lot of dirt and oil.

When washing by hand, put the pillow in a deep tub half full of warm water and a very generous quantity of suds. A plumber's plunger can be used to push suds and water in and out rather than using your hands. When the water is dirty, remove the pillow, change the water, add more soap or detergent and repeat the procedure.

Whether machine or hand washing, rinse thoroughly! You might want to run them through a second series of rinse cycles in the machine. If hand washing, use the same plunger method for rinsing, changing the water frequently until no more suds come out.

Squeeze out as dry as possible. Sew ripped seams. Dry in the drier on low or hang outdoors on a breezy day. As the pillows dry, shake and punch them occasionally to speed the drying process and make them fluffy. To determine if pillows are fully dry, weigh before washing, then weigh when you think they're dry and compare the two weights. If pillows are not fully dry, they will weigh more than they did before washing.

Fur—fake and genuine

To remove surface soil from both fake and real fur, rub either cornmeal or French chalk (available at many drugstores and recommended for white fur) into the fur gently. Then brush out thoroughly.

A fairly durable fake fur can be cleaned by sponging with a soft cloth dampened first with water and then with a few drops of ammonia. Go over the soiled areas to maintain a fresh look between professional cleanings.

Leather

In general, leather should be professionally cleaned. However, there are some relatively safe first aid treatments for certain common spot problems.

To remove mud stains from leather, gently wash the surface with a soft cloth that has been moistened with suds. Pat dry with a clean cloth. Dust with baby powder to close the pores of the leather and then buff with a clean dry cloth.

To remove mildew from leather, brush thoroughly and then wipe with a mild vinegar solution or diluted alcohol.

Plastic curtains and tablecloths

There are two kinds of plastic curtains: fairly heavy durable shower curtains and quite delicate plastic window curtains. The flimsier type can be washed in the washing machine, but be sure to set it on the gentle cycle and use warm water to keep the plastic pliable. Do not run more than two or four minutes. Never put these through a wringer, but shake off excess water and put in the drier to tumble or air fluff with no heat since the heat could melt the plastic. Such curtains can be line dried or wiped dry if preferred.

More durable plastic shower curtains can be machine washed in fairly hot water. Add a couple of towels along with the curtains. The action of the towels tumbling against the curtain will help remove mildew and dirt. A cup of white vinegar added to the hot rinse water will help keep the curtains soft and pliable.

Plastic tablecloths can be washed like shower curtains. Or clean them with sudsy water and a plastic bristle brush.

Silk

Many 100-percent silk garments are labeled "dry-clean only." In this case, you are far safer to follow those instructions. However, silk, since it is a natural fiber, can often be washed. The safest procedure for washing silk is to hand launder it, using a cold-water detergent specially formulated for delicate hand-washable fabrics.

Wool

These tips came from an experienced spinner, and can be used on most *colorfast* woollen knit and woven wool fabrics. The most important thing to remember when washing wool is to keep the temperature of the wash water and the rinse water the same. Best results are obtained with cool water and a concentrated liquid washing compound designed for woollens and fine hand washables.

The fabric should be gently pressed by hand, pushing the water through the fibers, and never agitated while washing. Water should never be allowed to run directly onto the fabric. Add garments to the water after the basin is filled.

When "wringing out," do not wring, but press and squeeze to remove the excess water. Do not lift the garment up while it is heavy with the water in it or the garment will stretch. Press the water out against the sides of the basin. Wool has tiny hooks or scales on it and unless all the above directions are followed carefully, these hooks will come together and "felt" the wool.

The squeezed-out garment can be put in the washer, set on delicate cycle, and spin dried to get the rest of the water out. Or, you can roll the garment into a thick towel, pressing to get out as much water as possible. Too much moisture left in the fabric will slow drying and may cause spotting.

Finally, lay it flat to dry or put on a plastic hanger making sure the garment does not stretch at the neck, shoulders or sleeves. Never hang such a garment unless most of the moisture is out.

CHAPTER 2

Cleaning Clothing Accessories

Gloves

After washing gloves, insert a clothespin into each finger and thumb to hold their shape while drying.

Felt hats

To clean any felt hats, including Stetsons and cowboy hats, rub with one of the following cleaners, then brush well.
Equal parts flour, salt and cornmeal
Coarse pickling salt
Pieces of stale rye bread
Upholstery cleaner

Knit hats and bonnets

Delicate knitted hats such as angora baby bonnets can stretch or shrink if not handled with care. Wash by hand in cold water and a liquid detergent formulated for woollens and fine hand washables. Be careful not to let the bonnet stretch, but squeeze water and suds through it gently. Rinse and press out the clear water in the same manner. Put the damp bonnet over an appropriately sized bowl to dry, gently pushing it into shape. Air dry at normal room temperature. Cold air from a hair drier can be used to fluff up the angora after it is completely dry.

To dry-clean a delicate knitted hat, gently rub flour or cornmeal into the fabric, then shake out thoroughly.

After washing any knitted cap or hat, stuff with tissue paper to hold the proper shape while it dries.

Straw or panama hats

Entirely cover the hat with a thick paste made of laundry starch and water. Dry in the sun, then brush thoroughly. Use only enough water to make a thick paste, since the hat must not be saturated with water.

Shoes and Handbags

Boots

Salt and water stains can be removed from boots with either vinegar or rubbing alcohol. Wipe on over the stained area only, then polish.

Remove old accumulated salt stains as follows: Wipe leather with a flannel cloth dipped in milk. Then rub saddle soap into the leather, and wipe away any residue with a clean soft cloth. If leather is dried and cracked, use a leather conditioning dressing available in hardware stores and shoe repair shops.

When lined rubber boots get damp on the inside, dry them quickly and easily with a hair drier.

Keep a long handled brush by an outdoor water faucet, in the mud room, or outside the entrance to your house. Use for cleaning mud off boots and overshoes.

Canvas and nylon   After machine washing canvas shoes, push a nice smooth rock into each toe before putting the shoes on a rack to dry to keep the shoe from shrinking. No more pinched toes.

Even though most canvas shoes and bags can be machine washed, persistent spots and allover dirt do not always come entirely clean. Here are some effective cleaning methods:

To get canvas tennis shoes really white, wet them, then sprinkle with a household cleanser containing bleach. Scrub well with a hand brush. Rinse well and wipe dry, then allow to dry in the sun to finish bleaching.

Clean colored canvas with detergent suds and a nail brush. Scrub well (the nail brush will be small enough to clean in tiny areas and around trim), then repeat with clear water to remove suds.

Some sport shoes combine canvas or nylon with real suede and leather and cannot be washed. Clean the fabric with upholstery foam spray, following directions on the can. Treat leather or suede areas just as you would an all leather shoe. Of course, imitation suede made of nylon or a similar fiber can be washed.

Leather

After polishing white shoes, rub them well with waxed paper. Smudges will wipe off easily with a damp cloth or paper towel after this treatment and the shoes will stay white much longer.

Petroleum jelly rubbed into shoes after polishing will provide a soft shine and keep the leather pliable.

Permanent scuff marks on white shoes can be touched up with white ink. For shoes with a glossy finish like patent leather or vinyl, apply a bit of clear nail polish over the dried ink to preserve the shine.

When you don't have time to polish white shoes, try rubbing scuff marks with an alcohol swab.

An ordinary pencil eraser will remove many marks from light-colored leather.

To touch up colored shoes, dab scuff marks and scratches with food coloring on a cotton swab. Then polish with neutral paste polish. Food coloring, of course, can be mixed to achieve the appropriate shade.

Patent, vinyl and plastic

Shine patent leather shoes and bags (and imitation patent, too) by applying petroleum jelly with a soft cloth, then buff.

Toothpaste will often remove black marks from patent leather and similar materials. Put a little of the toothpaste on a damp cloth, rub lightly, buff with a soft clean cloth. If marks prove too stubborn for this treatment, try putting a little baking soda on the cloth with the toothpaste.

A cotton ball dampened with nail-polish remover is excellent for removing black scuff marks from shiny white vinyl. However, do not try this on regular-colored leather. It may remove both the color and finish.

Ball-point ink marks can be removed with hair spray. The spray dissolves the ink and when it "bleeds," just wipe it away with a damp cloth.

Spray furniture polish provides a quick touch-up for plastic shoes and bags. Rub with soft cloths or paper towels.

Touch up composition soles and heels with a black or brown felt-tip pen, which lasts longer than polish and is easier to apply.

Sprinkle suede shoes and bags with talcum powder, then **Suede** brush well. Special wire suede brushes are available for this, but a regular medium bristle brush will also work.

Suede can be given an allover cleaning by rubbing lightly with fine sandpaper.

Rubbing alcohol will also clean light-colored suede. Be careful not to saturate the leather, but use a light hand. Do test in an inconspicious spot first; there is the chance that the alcohol may remove some colors.

CHAPTER 3

Drying, Ironing, and Other Laundry Problems

Bleeding colors   Deeply colored articles like new towels, blue jeans or vividly colored sheets should be washed alone for the first several washes to avoid staining other fabrics with running dye. The following are some old-fashioned remedies to set colors and eliminate or shorten the bleeding of the dye.

Add 1 cup of white vinegar to each gallon of rinse water.

Soak in a saltwater solution or add a handful of table salt to the wash cycle of your machine.

Soak in a solution of 1 tablespoon alum to each quart of water.

Drying

Electric and gas clothes driers are marvelous, indispensable time and work savers, but hanging your wash out on a sunny day can save energy and cut utility bills, give the family's clothes a fresh, clean scent and brighten white fabrics. There are also some fabrics that can be damaged by high drier temperatures and must be naturally air dried. Here are some pointers for making line and natural drying easier and problem free.

Keep an old cotton glove in your clothespin bag. Before using your clothesline, put on the glove and quickly run your hand over the line to remove dirt and dust.

Clip small items like bras, briefs and socks to wire coat hangers, then just hook the hanger over the line. This is also handy to hook over a rod or hook in the bathroom or laundry room.

After washing slacks and trousers, hang them by the legs. The weight of the set garment will remove almost all wrinkles and they will need little pressing.

When line drying clothes in cold weather, wipe the clothesline with a cloth dampened with vinegar to prevent the clothes from freezing and sticking to the line.

When hanging sheer or lightweight curtains or sheets, clip clothespins across the bottom of the item to weigh it down.

This will prevent wrinkles and keep large items from wrapping around the line on breezy days.

Large bedspreads and draperies can stretch in the middle where they are draped and pinned over the clothesline. To prevent this, drape such things over a widely spaced double line and do not use clothespins. Or, pin both top and bottom edges to the line with the center fold at the bottom, rather than over the line.

Put freshly washed shirts and blouses on padded hangers before hanging them to dry. Instead of pinning the shirt to the line, hook the hanger over the line instead. Shirts dry with fewer wrinkles and without stretching out of shape.

On a windy day, hangers can be kept from blowing off the line by hooking them through a rubber canning-jar ring that you've slipped over the clothesline.

While hanging out the family laundry, clip a snap clothespin on any garment where it needs mending or repair. This saves time looking for holes and rips later.

When hanging pleated curtains, clip the pleats in with clothespins to hold in place.

An empty plastic jug is handy for holding clothespins. Cut a hole high up in the side large enough to reach into and string the jug handle on your clothesline. It's easy to slide along the line as you work, keeping pins within reach.

A handful of table salt added to the final rinse water will keep clothes from freezing when you hang them out on a cold day.

Heavy sweaters that must be laid flat to dry can take several days when spread out on a table. You can make a quick-dry rack for such items by cleaning a window screen and placing it across two chairs. Shape the sweater on the screen and leave it to dry. The air can reach it from the bottom as well as the top to speed drying.

Place a plastic dry-cleaner's bag on the floor under drying racks such as that described above. It will prevent water spots on floor or carpet.

A more permanent drying table can be made by cutting out the top of a card table and fastening wire screening over it.

Hang a nonstretching sweater to dry without leaving clothespin marks by putting a towel through the armholes and fastening the towel ends to the clothesline.

To drip-dry blouses, shirts or other garments on metal, unpadded hangers, fold one or two paper towels over the ends of each hanger to prevent marks on the garments.

Use a discarded paper-towel roll to prevent horizontal creases in garments like slacks that are hung over the bottoms of wire coat hangers. Slit the tube lengthwise and place it over the wire bar of the hanger, then tape the slit shut.

Very small items can be quickly dried with a hand-held blow drier.

Panty hose hung to drip-dry can stretch and lose that perfect fit from the weight of the water running down the length of the hose. To avoid the problem, let them dry flat on a bath towel. They will still dry overnight and fit like new.

If you have a gas oven with a pilot light, tennis shoes and small articles can be stretched over the oven rack to dry overnight.

Ironing and Wrinkle Control

In grandmother's house, Monday was wash day and Tuesday was ironing day. Today's miracle permanent-press fabrics have ended much of the drudgery of ironing, but wrinkles can still be a problem. Try some of the following pointers to make your Tuesdays (or any ironing day) easier.

To remove wrinkles set in by a too-hot washing or drying cycle, soak a pressing cloth with a solution of half water and half white vinegar and wring out. Place this over the wrinkled fabric and press with a rather hot iron. Remove the pressing cloth and let the iron cool down to the appropriate temperature for the fabric you're treating, then press the garment dry. If this doesn't completely eliminate wrinkles, repeat the process using full-strength white vinegar.

Another way to use the same treatment given above is to fill your steam iron with the water and vinegar solution, then press as usual.

Many wrinkles can be avoided by removing clothes from the drier while still very slightly damp. Hang carefully on padded hangers. They will finish air drying very quickly.

Liquid spray starch is very effective in removing wrinkles and heavy creases left by lengthening hemlines. Follow directions on the can and press at the proper temperature for your fabric.

Wrinkles and creases from packaged bedpreads and drapes can be removed by putting them in the drier with a large damp bath towel. Set the drier on warm (not hot) and let them tumble for about ten minutes. This is also effective for removing creases from plastic tablecloths and shower curtains.

To avoid having to iron large drapes or curtains after washing, try the following laundering method. Fold the soiled curtains neatly as you remove then from the windows and keep them folded through each step. Soak in a dry all-fabric bleach and warm water and press down with the hands to force the soil from the fabric. Next follow the same procedure using detergent and warm water. Rinse using the same procedure and several changes of clear water. Then place the still folded curtains in the bottom of the empty automatic washer and run them through the spin-dry cycle only. Remove while damp/dry, and hang them back at the windows to finish air drying.

Napped fabrics such as velvet or velour cannot easily be pressed without destroying the texture and appearance of the fabric. To remove wrinkles, hang in a closed bathroom while you run very hot water from the tub faucet. When wrinkles have disappeared (it should only take five minutes or so) allow the garment to drip-dry since it will be quite damp from the steam. This technique is also very handy to use while traveling. It works on many fabrics.

Those who travel with a curling iron for their hair can use it as an emergency iron as well.

A brown paper bag dampened with water makes an adequate emergency substitute for a regular pressing cloth.

To speed up all ironing, put a wide strip of heavy-duty aluminum foil under your ironing board cover. As you iron, the heat will be reflected and the ironing will not only go faster, but be more effective since you're "ironing" on both sides of the fabric at once.

Anyone who sews knows that pressing open seams can be one of the most difficult and tedious ironing jobs. A handy way to speed up the job is to keep an ice cube in a dish nearby as you work. Use the ice cube to run up and down the seams before pressing. This eliminates messy spray bottles or having to wet more of the garment than necessary.

A length of nylon net put in the drier will remove lint from knits—about a yard will do. It can be reused indefinitely.   **Lint**

To remove human and animal hair, put garment in the drier set on cool or no-heat.

To prevent lint from accumulating on clothes while laundering, turn garments inside out. This also helps stop fading.

Lint and "pilling" can be lightly shaved off knits with a clean disposable razor.

To make an easy-to-use lint remover, wrap masking tape around an empty bathroom tissue roll, sticky side out. Just roll it along the linty clothes. When the tape loses its "grip," just cover with another layer of tape.

Here are a few remedies to "unshrink" wool.   **Shrunken wool**

Boil garment gently in 1 part vinegar and 2 parts water for twenty-five minutes. Reblock to original shape and size before air drying.

Wash in cool water, then try to stretch to original size. Lay flat to dry, stretching again when almost dry.

Rinse the garment or blanket several times. Stiffness and shrinking in wool can be aggravated by soap residue in an improperly rinsed item. In your washer, prepare a solution of 1 cup of white vinegar to each gallon of water, then gently wash article in this solution. Spin dry, pull into shape and line dry.

Stiffness

To soften stiff new blue jeans, wash the jeans two or three times before they are worn, adding about 2 cups of liquid bleach to a washer of clear water. The bleach must be added and well mixed with the water *before* the jeans are put into the washer or they may come out splotched with bleach stains. Add fabric softener to the last washing.

Another remedy for stiff new jeans is to soak them overnight in water mixed with a cup of salt.

Terry towels, washcloths and dish towels can become hard and stiff if they are not thoroughly rinsed. Use detergent only in the prewash or soak cycle and let the wash and subsequent rinse cycles run with clear water only. Tumble dry on medium heat, remove towels as soon as they are dry and shake to fluff them.

If you have a clothes drier but like to save energy by line drying, the stiffness that sometimes affects air-dried clothes can be eliminated by hanging the clothes until almost dry, then tumbling in the drier for only a few minutes.

To keep plastic tablecloths and curtains pliable when washing, add a couple of tablespoons of glycerine to the final rinse water.

You can make your own fabric softener sheets for use in the drier by dampening a paper towel with regular fabric softener. Just toss in the drier as you would with the commercial product.

CHAPTER 4

Cleaning All Around the House

I saw on TV some lady like me
Wash her walls with a magic cleaner.
It melted the grime in record time,
So effortless her demeanor.
I rushed to the store, bought bottles galore,
But scrubbed 'til my elbows hurt.
The product's the same—I bought it by
    name;
I must have the wrong kind of dirt.

                    Edith Z.

If this little verse, sent in by a reader, reflects your own frustration with cleaning, take heart. You don't need to buy dozens of specialized cleaning products to keep everything in your home fresh and sparkling; most chores can be easily accomplished by using common household products you already have, plus the know-how found in these cleaning pointers.

Fireplaces

Fireplaces, by their very nature, are prone to become dirty. Soot and smoke stain the bricks or stones, and if you do any cooking in your fireplace, you may have to cope with grease spatters as well. Here are a number of cleaning compounds to try on your fireplace. Whichever you use, *always rinse thoroughly* afterward.

Scrub with a strong solution of washing soda and water with a stiff brush. Steel wool and scouring powder also work well.

Apply a paste of concentrated ammonia and powdered pumice. Leave this mixture on for a couple of hours, then scrub with a stiff brush and hot water.

Scrub with cider vinegar and a stiff brush. Blot with a sponge or paper towel, then rub with a towel that has been dipped in clear water.

Add 4 ounces yellow laundry soap to enough hot water to make a quart of soft soap. Heat until soap dissolves, cool and then stir in ½ pound powdered pumice stone and ½ cup household ammonia. After mixing well, scrub stones with a stiff brush. Use a clean brush to apply another coat of the cleaning mixture and leave it on about fifteen minutes, then scrub off with the brush and clean warm water. Rinse with more clear water.

Scrub with equal parts liquid bleach and water.

Spray a heavy coat of oven cleaner on the bricks, let it stand a while, then rinse off with water and a sponge. Be sure to protect the surrounding area, including your floor, carpet and adjoining wall from the cleaner by covering with newspaper or plastic.

Once you've got those bricks or stones clean, apply a coat of linseed oil. It helps maintain the beauty of unpainted brick, stone and slate and makes them easier to clean.

Fireplace doors   To remove the brown baked-on film from glass fireplace doors, remove the doors and place them flat. Lay paper towels over the stained areas and pour full-strength ammonia on the towels. Let it stand about five minutes and the heaviest soil will wipe away quickly.

A spray-foam bathroom tub and tile cleaner will also clean fireplace doors. Just spray on and when the bubbles start to dissolve, the brown sludge will soften and can be wiped away.

Another formula that will loosen the film is toothpaste on a soft bristle brush along with a cleaner that has ammonia in it.

For an old-fashioned but absolutely free cleaner for those glass doors, dip a damp cloth in cold wood ashes and rub on the glass. After rinsing, you can go over them with a glass cleaner or vinegar and water to add a pretty shine.

Floors

Black heel marks

Moisten a clean cloth or sponge and sprinkle it with baking soda. Rub gently on spots and rinse with water.

Rub marks with a little toothpaste on a paper towel, then rinse.

An ordinary pencil eraser will remove many black heel marks from vinyl floors.

Dust

To clean dust and dirt from under or behind heavy appliances like the refrigerator, stove, washer or drier, wrap a sponge or cloth around a yardstick and fasten in place with a rubber band.

A fast and easy way to dust baseboards without bending: Put on a pair of old thick cotton socks and just run your toes around the dusty edges.

Food stains

Rub lightly with a cloth that has been dipped in rubbing alcohol, then rinse. If your floor is not the no-wax variety, apply a self-polishing wax or a one-step clean and polish wax.

Rubbing alcohol added to the rinse water after washing floors with detergent cleaners will also remove any sticky soap residue from the floor.

Paint spots

Full-strength vinegar rubbed on with a cloth will remove some latex paint spots. The older the spot is, the harder you will have to rub.

A piece of nylon net can be used to rub paint spots away with minimal damage to the finish of the floor or woodwork.

Steel wool will usually remove paint spots, but it will also remove wax. You can touch up those spots with a little floor wax to preserve the wood between regular waxings.

Rust

Rust spots are sometimes left on floors from the bottoms of stoves, refrigerators or metal cabinets. To remove such spots, make a solution of oxalic acid and water and apply with a non-woven nylon pad. When stains are removed, use the same pad with a floor cleaner, rinse, and then apply your usual floor finish. Oxalic acid is poisonous and very strong, so wear rubber gloves and use extreme care.

An alternate method for using oxalic acid on rust spots is to tie the crystals in a piece of cheesecloth, dampen this little bag and apply to the stains. As above, when stain is removed, rinse thoroughly with clear water. Remember to wear rubber gloves.

Tiles To remove floor tiles, put a piece of an old sheet or similar cloth over two or three tiles and iron over them until they become warm. This should soften the glue enough so that you can pry them up with a putty knife. Only work on two or three at a time, because they will restick if they have time to cool.

You can also use a blow drier to help remove tiles. Start at one corner and hold the drier (set on high) about two or three inches above the tile. This will warm and soften the adhesive enough to peel back the corner. Move the drier back and forth over the unheated portion of the tile as you slowly peel off the heated portion.

Wax buildup Pour a little turpentine on the area to be cleaned and then rub with steel wool. Wipe up the "goop" before going to the next area. Work on only a small area at a time. When you have gone over the entire floor in this manner, wash it with warm mild soapsuds and rinse with clear warm water. Use as little water as possible and dry thoroughly. This treatment can be used on hardwood floors or linoleum.

To remove wax buildup on vinyl tile or linoleum floors, mix a solution of 1 cup of ammonia, 1 cup of detergent and one gallon of warm water. Apply the solution liberally with a sponge mop and leave for from three to five minutes. Then scrub with a stiff brush or fine steel wool (do not use steel wool on high gloss vinyl). Remove the solution with a mop or cloth. Work on a small area at a time and proceed area by area until entire floor is stripped of wax. Rinse with clear, cool water. If any wax film remains, repeat the stripping on spots where needed and rinse. Dry thoroughly before applying new wax. Older floors may require two coats of wax after stripping to attain the desired gloss.

For a nice shiny finish when cleaning your no-wax vinyl floor, add a small amount of a presoak laundry powder to your sudsy water.

Rugs and Carpets

General cleaning tips

Use an old toothbrush to clean corners and edges of carpets that are easily missed with the vacuum or rug shampooer.

After shampooing a carpet, remove excess water easily by rolling it with a clean paint roller, then absorbing the excess water that comes to the surface with a sponge mop or towels.

After shampooing a carpet that is likely to be walked on while still damp, spread heavy old bath towels on the damp carpet.

They will help soak up moisture as well as keep the carpet clean while it dries.

Special Problems

Whenever you spill anything on a rug or carpet, blot it up as quickly as possible. Stains are much less likely to remain if you act while the spill is fresh. Use paper towels to firmly blot up the substance, changing towels frequently until most of the liquid is absorbed. Do not rub—that will only work the dirt into the fibers. The following are pointers for dealing with specific problems.

Beverage stains

This procedure is the same for most beverage stains including fruit juice, soft drinks, tea or wine. Sponge with lukewarm water, then with a neutral (nonalkaline without added bleach) detergent solution of 2 teaspoons detergent to 2 cups warm water. Blot up and rinse by sponging in clear water. If stain remains, mix ¼ cup white vinegar with ¾ cup water and apply with a dampened cloth. Leave on about fifteen minutes, blot and rinse. Use the damp cloth in the direction of the pile during the final blotting.

Bleach spots

Light spots on carpets caused by spilling bleach or using various cleaning solutions on stains are best touched up by a professional rug drier. However, if the spots are very small, you might try the following with a home dye. Dampen the spot so the dye will penetrate. Then apply the warm dye with a toothbrush, or drop on with a medicine dropper or artist's paintbrush. Brush all through the fibers going from the center out so it is blended into the adjoining color.

Blood

A fresh blood stain can be rubbed lightly with an ice cube, then blotted up with a paper towel.

Sponge dried bloodstains with cold water, then apply with a medicine dropper a solution made of 2 teaspoons detergent (nonalkaline and without bleach) into 2 cups of warm water. If a yellow stain appears after this treatment, apply a few drops of hydrogen peroxide and allow to remain for two or three minutes. Sponge with cold water. Blot up as much excess moisture as possible with folded cloths or paper towels.

Candle wax

Scrape off as much of the wax as you can with a dull knife without tearing the carpet fibers. Often the remainder can be removed with a nonflammable dry-cleaning fluid. If not, cover the remaining wax with paper towels. Press over the towels with a warm iron. Be sure to change towels when any wax has been transferred to the paper. If this is not done, the warm iron will just put it back into the rug nap. Keep changing towels and pressing over them until no more wax appears on the paper. If any color stain remains after all the wax is removed, sponge again with cleaning fluid.

An alternative method is to hold a blow drier over the wax until the heat melts it, then blot up with paper towels. Again, if a color stain remains, sponge with dry-cleaning fluid.

Chewing gum

Put an ice cube or two (enough to cover) onto the gum for about ten minutes, then remove the ice and gently lift the gum from the surface. Any residue can be generally cleaned up with a very light sprinkling of lighter fluid. Sponge *thoroughly* with water to rinse as lighter fluid is, of course, flammable.

Furniture indentations

Use the edge of a coin or a plastic credit card to push the pile back into place. Then hold your steam iron about three or four inches above the mark and the hot steam should raise the pile.

Another solution is to wring a clean white cloth out of hot water and spread it over the spots. Leave on ten minutes or so and then brush the carpet against the nap with a stiff scrub brush. When the carpet is dry, brush with the nap.

Grease and oil

Apply a nonflammable dry-cleaning fluid and blot with a clean white cloth until the cloth no longer picks up any stain. If any spots remain, try a mixture of ¼ cup white vinegar in ¾ cup water. Apply to area and pat with a clean cloth. Leave about fifteen minutes, blot and rinse with a clean cloth moistened with warm water. Sponge in the direction of the pile and blot again with a clean cloth.

Plain cornmeal will soak up a fresh grease or oil stain. Pour on a generous amount, gently stamp it into the fibers and leave overnight. Next morning, brush or vacuum it out.

Pet stains

Fresh urine or other stains left by pets should be immediately doused with club soda.

Older stains should be treated first with several applications of lukewarm water (you may add a teaspoon of detergent to a cup of water if the stain is very bad) that is then absorbed with a clean cloth. Then squeeze on a solution of ½ cup white vinegar mixed with 1½ cups lukewarm water. Absorb and dry thoroughly with a pad of paper towels or cloth. Proceed with caution. While this is effective in most cases, occasionally you may see some color change in the affected area. In that case, the only way to restore these spots is by spot dyeing, best done by a professional.

Resin or sap

This is a common Christmas stain, or one you may have a problem with if you bring logs into the house for your fireplace. Foaming bathroom cleaner rubbed in by hand will dissolve the resin and remove stickiness. Sponge over the area with a damp cloth after the spot is removed.

Sheepskin rugs

Sheep- and lambskins can be washed in the machine. Use cold or lukewarm water, a very mild detergent and very gentle agitation. Be sure the skins are rinsed thoroughly. Dry flat indoors or in the shade outdoors. Shake occasionally while drying to fluff up the fibers, then brush with an ordinary hairbrush when the rug is dry.

To dry-clean a sheepskin or fur rug, sprinkle generously with cornmeal, then shake out as much as possible and brush out the remainder.

Static electricity

To eliminate static buildup from a carpet, especially a nylon one, mix a quart of fabric softener in 2 gallons of water and spray it on the carpet heavily enough so that it is noticeably wet. Allow carpet to dry and static will be prevented for three to four months.

Tar

When tar is fresh, gently scrape up as much as possible. Then apply a dry-cleaning solution and follow with solution of 1 teaspoon white vinegar in a quart of warm water. Reapply dry-cleaning fluid, dry and then brush the pile gently. Do not oversaturate the rug and dry as quickly as possible.

Walls

Walls—especially in homes with young children—seem to act like a magnet for every imaginable kind of dirt. Grease spatters them, children draw on them, smoke from cigarettes, candles and fireplaces turn them brown and dingy. These pointers should help you find ways to keep your walls, paneling, wallpaper and woodwork fresher and brighter.

General washing and cleaning

When washing painted plaster walls, avoid strong cleansers. A good detergent should remove average soil. First dust off any loose dirt and then use a sponge or soft cloth to wash in a circular motion. Start at the bottom and work up to avoid streaks.

An old nylon sweater (cut the buttons off) is a great wall-washing rag. The nylon just seems to glide along.

When washing enclosed stair walls, start at the bottom step and work up. You'll feel much safer working since this procedure gives you a tendency to lean forward toward the incline and there is less chance of losing your balance and falling.

You can easily make an excellent wall duster by attaching a large pompon of nylon net to a long piece of doweling. Excellent for removing cobwebs in ceiling corner. You might also try running it over your carpet for an emergency lint removal job when you've no time to vacuum.

The area around light switches is particularly prone to smudges and fingerprints. To cut down on this problem, remove the switchplate, clean the area around the switch and then apply a thin coat of clear shellac. The wall switch area will then be easy to clean with a quick swish with a damp cloth.

Special Problems

Rub toothpaste on crayon marks, then rinse off with clear water.

Crayon marks

Baking soda on a damp rag, full strength, will also remove crayon marks. This also works on pencil and some pen marks.

Before removing mildew, and to prevent its recurrence, the room must be made as dry as possible. An auxiliary heater in the problem area will help. In closets, a small electric lightbulb should be left on (be sure it is not too close to clothes or any other objects). After the room is dry, the mildew spots should be carefully wiped off, then wiped with a cloth moistened with denatured alcohol.

Mildew

Poor circulation can be a cause of mildew on walls. A small electric fan placed near the room's heating vent should help. Place the fan as high as possible and aim downward.

Before painting a room with a mildew problem, you must remove as much mold as possible. Some mold will remain in the plaster or wall material, so shellac the wall before painting, then use a mildew-resistant paint.

Many spots—grease, oil, water spots, ink marks, etc.— will bleed through paint no matter how many coats you use. To prevent this, cover such spots with hair spray or clear fingernail polish. Let dry thoroughly before painting.

Painting tips

To remove water-base paint from light switchplates safely, remove the wall plates and then soak them in hot water with detergent powder added. The paint will loosen in a few minutes and it can easily be removed with a stiff brush.

Paneling and woodwork

Use the following solution to clean wood paneling. Mix 1 tablespoon white vinegar and 1 tablespoon olive oil in a quart of warm water. Wring a cloth out of this and use it to rub down the paneling. Dry with a clean soft cloth and when thoroughly dry, apply a thin coat of paste wax, then buff. A tablespoon of turpentine can be substituted for the vinegar.

Dull and scratched paneling can be revived with a commercial scratch-removing polish. Wipe it in and off a small area at a time. Dip a cotton swap in this polish to get into larger nicks and holes.

Another touch-up for scratches in paneling is paste shoe polish. Select the shade closest to that of your paneling, rub it in well and buff to a luster.

When washing woodwork, use an old toothbrush to clean corners and crevices.

Smoke

To clean areas blackened by smoke from kerosene heaters, oil lamps and the like, try a solution of borax, ammonia and water. Add 2 ounces of borax and 1 teaspoon ammonia to 2 quarts of water. Work on only a small area at a time, rinse as you work and wipe off with an old terry towel or other soft thick cloth.

To remove grease spots on wallpaper, try applying a paste made of cornstarch and water. Leave on until dry, then brush off.

Wall paper

Clean vinyl wall coverings with baking soda on a damp sponge. A very light spray of window cleaner is also effective. Flocked wallpaper patterns can be particularly difficult to clean. Once flocking has become discolored, it is almost impossible to restore it to its former color. One solution is to paint over the wallpaper, flocking and all. The flocked pattern will, of course, still provide an interesting textured pattern even if the wall is now all one color.

Flocked patterns on a vinyl background can be dyed successfully with home fabric dye. Mix up a bucketful of dye solution at one time (enough for the entire job), apply to the flocking with a sponge and blot up the excess that forms at the edges of the patterns. Only the flocking takes on the new color. The vinyl background remains the same.

To remove wallpaper, wet the walls from the top down with warm water and a soft scrub brush. Be sure the paper is saturated all the way down a wide strip about a yard across. It may need wetting a second time to go through all layers if multiple layers of wallpaper have been applied. When it seems loose, use a putty knife to start loosening each strip and the paper will usually start to fall off in big pieces. When most of the paper is off, remove all the small clinging bits while they are still wet. A nylon net scrubber is excellent for rubbing off all these tiny pieces.

For an even speedier job, use a paint roller dipped in steaming hot water. Just roll it along one strip of paper at a time and in most cases the paper will peel right off.

Windows

Nine Window-Washing Formulas

1. One-half cup ammonia and ⅛ cup vinegar mixed into 1 quart water.

2. One-fourth cup nonsudsing ammonia, 2 tablespoons of alcohol and 2 cups water. Put in a spray bottle, spray on and wipe well with clean lint-free cloth.

3. One tablespoon vinegar mixed into 1 quart water. Use crinkled newspapers for wiping and drying.

4. One-fourth cup cornstarch in 2 quarts warm water.

5. Automobile windshield cleaner (available in inexpensive gallon jugs) mixed half and half with water.

6. One tablespoon fabric softener and 1 tablespoon cornstarch added to one quart water.

7. One-half cup denatured alcohol in 2 quarts of warm water. This is particularly effective in winter to prevent windows from frosting up.

8. To prevent windows from fogging up, pour liquid soap on a paper towel or rag and wipe over windows.

9. A soft cloth dipped in spirits of camphor is very effective for cleaning greasy windows, mirrors or picture glass.

After washing windows, dry them on the inside with a sideways motion and on the outside with an up and down motion. If there are any streaks remaining, you will know immediately whether they are on the inside or the outside of the window.

Adhesive marks

To remove sticky residue left on windows from tape or adhesive paper, rub with warm white vinegar or nail-polish remover. For tough spots, rub with a brush or a ball of nylon net.

Hardened cement

Blobs of hardened cement or concrete on windows must be carefully scraped off with a razor blade, but the job will be easier if you rub the spots generously with mineral oil first.

Windows that stick

When you clean windows, wipe paste wax up and down their tracks to make them slide easier. If windows seem permanently stuck, pour liquid soap down each side. This should provide sufficient lubrication to make them work again.

CHAPTER 5

Cleaning Furniture

Brass To clean and polish solid brass, mix salt, vinegar and enough flour to make a thin paste. Rub well onto the brass with a soft cloth, rinse thoroughly after cleaning and dry well. If there are any green spots on the brass, dip a cloth in a weak solution of ammonia and water, dry immediately and then proceed with cleaning.

To remove heavy black tarnish from brass, prepare a solution of lemon juice and salt. Rub in with extra-fine steel wool, rinse well and dry thoroughly. For a final finish, let the piece stand in the sun for an hour or so, then coat with tung oil and allow to dry.

To prevent brass from tarnishing, after cleaning spray it with a clear lacquer formulated for use on metal.

Many modern brass items are not solid brass, but merely brass plated and should not be polished with brass polish. They generally are already coated with a factory-applied lacquer finish. To keep these pieces looking bright, just dust regularly and periodically buff them with paste wax.

Chinese lacquer

To remove water rings, heat marks and other stains from lacquered furniture, mix powdered pumice and linseed oil and rub on the marks. Wipe off with a soft clean cloth.

Black lacquered pieces can also be washed with a strong solution of tea, wiped dry with a soft clean cloth and shined to a high luster.

Dusting pointers

To shorten your dusting time, saturate two cotton work gloves with lemon oil or any furniture cream, put the gloves on and just rub your hands over, under and all around each piece of furniture. Fast and easy.

A one-inch soft paint brush sprayed with your favorite furniture polish is great for cleaning corners, carvings and other intricate places on furniture.

A cotton swab dipped in alcohol is handy for reaching under the dial when cleaning the telephone.

And how does one clean bedsprings on an old-fashioned bed? Try a moplike bottle washer. Just wet the washer and go to it. No more sore fingers from trying to maneuver a cloth around all those coils.

Marble

Wipe marble surfaces with a cloth wrung out of warm water and a mild detergent once or twice a year and they should stay in good shape. In between these washings, dust regularly and occasionally wipe with a damp cloth. Marble is somewhat porous and water can soak into it, so avoid frequent washing.

A coat of liquid furniture wax can be applied to marble to prevent staining.

To remove stains from marble, mix a thick paste of household cleanser and hot water. Spread generously over the stain, cover with a piece of plastic and leave for several days before removing by rinsing with lukewarm water. If this does not erase the stain, try soaking paper towels with peroxide or ammonia, apply, cover and leave for about twenty-four hours. Rinse with a damp cloth. After marks are gone, buff with a soft cloth and talcum powder.

To remove cigarette burns from marble and marble-type materials, use #600 grit wet, or dry sandpaper and water. Polish with a very fine polishing compound. These materials are, of course, available at most hardware stores.

Piano keys

If your piano is an old one, its keys may be real ivory. On the other hand, most modern pianos have plastic keys. Here's how to clean both types.

Soap will stain or darken real ivory. To clean, wipe the keys with a flannel cloth lightly moistened with denatured alcohol. Dry immediately with a clean flannel cloth.

Plastic keys can be cleaned with a cloth just moistened with lighter fluid. No rinsing is necessary. Be very careful not to wet the cloth so much that any liquid will drip between the keys.

Another cleaner for plastic piano keys is toothpaste and a soft cloth.

Upholstered and Fabric-Covered Furniture

In general, upholstered furniture can be adequately cleaned with upholstery shampoo and the various application methods with which it is sold. However, there are certain special fabrics which benefit from special treatment. Here are some pointers for some of the most common problems.

Lampshades

Many fabric lampshades can be washed, but try to test the fabric before proceeding to see if water will damage it. If any parts of the shade are glued, the glue might dissolve, so do be careful. Follow the procedure described below to wash lamp-shades.

Fill the bathtub higher than the depth of the shade with water and a detergent for delicate fabrics. Dunk the shade up and down in the suds, being sure it is completely immersed each time. Rub any stubborn spots with a soft brush. Repeat suds treatment if need be and then rinse three or four times in clear water—always being sure the entire shade is covered.

Blot the excess water with a towel. Tie a string to the top center of the shade frame and suspend it from a clothesline in the shade outside and preferably on a slightly breezy day so it will dry as quickly as possible. If this is not possible, hang the shade from the bathroom shower rod to drip-dry. Some fabrics may look stretched while wet but will tighten up as they dry.

Nonwashable lampshades such as parchment or fabric over stiff paper can be cleaned with dough-type wallpaper cleaner.

Pleated plastic lampshades are easily cleaned with a small foam paintbrush dipped in warm soapy water. Rinse the brush often and squeeze out as much water as you can so it is nearly dry when using it on the shade. The wedge shape fits into the pleats and does a terrific job.

Dust any type of pleated lampshade with a very soft brush. It's more thorough, faster and gentler to the shade than using a cloth.

Leather

The best way to clean leather furniture is with saddle soap. It is available as a spray for ease of application. Just spray it on, rub it off and the leather will stay soft and beautiful.

Mattresses

To remove bloodstains from mattresses, make a paste of laundry starch and water and apply thickly to the stains. Let dry, brush off and repeat if necessary.

Another remedy for bloodstains on mattresses is to pour on three-percent medicinal strength hydrogen peroxide. Use sparingly and pour only on the stain. You do not want the solution to soak the mattress. Allow to dry thoroughly, but no rinsing is necessary.

Urine and other stains can be removed with the following paste: Mix 1 part liquid bleach, 3 parts water and enough talcum powder to make a thick paste. Brush on stains thickly, let it dry, then brush out. Repeat until stain disappears. (Older, more severe stains can require more than one application.) It's best if this job can be done outdoors or in the garage since there will be a lot of powdery dust when the mattress is brushed.

Net playpen

This clever pointer is specifically directed at washing a baby's net-type playpen, but it would also be applicable to any sturdy fabric piece when the fabric cannot be removed from a rigid frame—perhaps a fabric screen or certain fabric sling-style chairs. Use two old tube socks as mittens and wash with detergent and bleach mixed in water. With one hand inside and the other outside, rub the net or fabric between the sock mittens with the soapy water. Rinse with clear water in the same way.

To remove oil spots from velvet, gently apply cornstarch to the spots, leave it on for an hour or so, then gently brush away. **Velvet**

You can remove other spots from velvet with dry-cleaning fluid. Use sparingly and apply with an eye dropper so as to contact the stained area only. Sponge with a clean soft white cloth. Brush gently with a very soft brush to restore the nap.

Velvet can be dusted quickly and easily by wiping very lightly with a slightly dampened cloth.

Plastics used for upholstery vary greatly in strength and quality, so abrasives and strong solvents should be avoided in cleaning these pieces. They should be washed in clear water, or mild detergent suds. **Vinyl and plastic**

Stains from beverages, food, etc., should be wiped off plastic or vinyl with a cloth dampened with alcohol, then rinsed with a cloth wrung out of clear water. Dry with a soft cloth.

Petroleum jelly will also remove many stains from vinyl and will help keep the material supple. Rub it into the stain and allow it to soften the stain for a few minutes, then wipe away with a clean dry cloth.

Ball-point ink can be removed by spraying with hair spray. Leave it on for a few minutes to dissolve the ink, then wipe away with a damp cloth. Never, never use nail-polish remover on vinyl or plastic.

Stickiness can be removed from vinyl furniture by rubbing in cornstarch with a cloth.

Wood

Masking tape

Remove masking tape by rubbing with an ice cube, then "balling" the remaining tape up with your fingers. Sponge what remains with detergent suds that have a tiny bit of ammonia added. Wipe off with a damp cloth or sponge, then dry immediately.

Paint spots

To remove dried paint spots from wood finishes, cover the spots with linseed oil and leave on until the paint softens. If spots are small, apply oil with an eye dropper. When soft, carefully scrape paint off with a dull knife or your fingernail. Wax or polish as usual.

Paper spots

To remove paper stuck to wood, wet the paper with either liquid furniture polish or vegetable oil and leave on over night. In the morning, rub paper off with a dry cloth.

Severe peeling or blisters on wood finish usually means the **Peeling finish** piece will have to be refinished. However, if the problem does not seem too bad, try soaking a cloth in benzine and rub the furniture until clean. Wipe dry. If this treatment restores the wood enough so that you don't think you need to do a complete refinishing job, use a spray cleaner and preserver (available where furniture polishes are sold) to prevent further damage.

Pine furniture may become sticky from sap in the knots of **Stickiness** the wood. Benzine or alcohol will remove the stickiness temporarily.

To wash wood furniture and remove built-up wax, prepare **Washing** a solution of 1 tablespoon linseed oil or olive oil, 1 tablespoon turpentine and 1 quart of hot water. Allow to cool, then wring a soft clean cloth out of the mixture and rub the furniture briskly along the grain of the wood. Repeat until all the dirt, old wax and polish are removed. Work on only a small area at a time, and immediately dry each area thoroughly with another clean soft cloth. For a final finish, apply a thin coat of paste wax and rub to a luster.

To remove white rings, water marks, and other spots and **Water spots** stains from finished wood furniture, make a paste of cold cigarette or cigar ashes and butter or margarine. Apply to the spot and rub vigorously along the wood grain with a soft cloth until the stain disappears. Wipe off excess with a clean cloth. The older or deeper the spot, the harder you will have to rub, but persevere! With a little elbow grease and determination, this remedy works remarkably well.

Other substances useful for removing stains on wood furniture are toothpaste rubbed on gently with a paper towel, oil of peppermint rubbed in with a soft cloth, or lemon extract used sparingly on a soft cloth and rubbed in gently.

Petroleum jelly rubbed on such spots can be left overnight, then rubbed off. This leaves a soft luster and the piece may not need additional polishing.

CHAPTER 6

Shiny Kitchen,
Sparkling Bath

Basin, Tub and Bowl

What household chores are more dreaded than scrubbing a greasy kitchen sink, scouring mineral deposits from the bathroom basin, or scraping adhesive vinyl appliques off the bathtub. Don't give up hope! There is a way to get these problem areas clean and sparkling without devoting your life to the job. Pick your problem and your solution from these essential pointers.

Faucets Give a quick shine to chrome faucets by polishing briefly with a cloth moistened with rubbing alcohol or club soda.

To remove tough, hardened mineral deposits on faucets and taps, wrap them with paper towels or cloths well soaked in white vinegar. Cover with plastic wrap to prevent evaporation. After an hour or two, the accumulation can be washed away with a soft brush or cloth. Rinse and rub dry.

An old toothbrush is ideal to use when cleaning around and under faucets and taps. Really gets into those hard-to-reach places.

Glass fiber sinks, showers and tubs

Never use harsh abrasives or steel wool on glass fiber fixtures. For general cleaning, use an ordinary, mild household detergent and a nylon or plastic net scrubber. Wiping the sink or tub dry after each use will prevent the buildup of water stains and soap scum.

Minor stains on glass fiber fixtures can usually be removed with household ammonia or bleach. Save these strong chemicals for an occasional cleaning only.

Baking soda rubbed on with a damp sponge will remove many stains from glass fiber fixtures easily and safely. Rub, rinse and dry.

If your glass fiber sink is losing its luster, you can restore it with automobile wax. Don't use this in the tub, however, as it will make the surface slippery.

Glass shower doors

For day-to-day cleaning, a strong solution of vinegar and water will keep glass shower doors sparkling.

For heavy soap film and scum, rub *carefully* with very fine steel wool (be careful not to scratch the glass). Wash with dishwasher detergent, then finish off with a vinegar and water or ammonia and water cleaning for a clear shine.

Lemon oil not only cleans soap scum off glass doors but also acts as a preventative for future buildup. Wet a paper towel with lemon oil and use it to wipe away the dirt and film. Dry thoroughly. The tiny bit of oil left on the glass will allow water and soap film to just roll off between cleanings.

Try using a paintbrush dipped in your cleaning solution when cleaning shower door rails.

Porcelain fixtures

To remove general discolorations and stains from tubs and basins, rub a mixture of hydrogen peroxide and baking soda on the spots, let dry and then wash the mixture and grime away.

Particularly stubborn stains can usually be removed with kerosene. Add a few drops of kerosene to your sudsy cleaning water for general cleaning. You can also rub kerosene directly on spots with a paper towel, then wash with hot sudsy water, rinse with hot water and rub dry. There will be an odor from the kerosene, but an open window for a couple of hours should dispel it.

A rubbing compound used to buff cars is useful for removing heavy mineral and water spots.

Rub petroleum jelly on stubborn spots. Leave it on for a couple of days, then wipe clean.

Most new porcelain fixtures are acid resistant. To remove rust stains from such fixtures, rub with a cut lemon or rub with vinegar. If any stain remains, apply a very weak solution of oxalic acid (caution: this is poisonous), *leave on for just a few seconds,* then rinse very thoroughly. If this is left on too long, the acid can damage the finish of the sink.

Catsup can also be rubbed onto rust stains on acid-resistant sinks.

Older porcelain fixtures may not have an acid-resistant finish. To remove rust or mineral stains in such cases, clean with a solution of one bar of naptha soap chipped into a gallon of hot water to which you have added ½ cup paint thinner or a cleaning solvent. This should not harm the finish.

Removing adhesive bathtub appliques

To remove those rubber or vinyl safety appliques so often used in tubs and showers, fill the tub or bottom of the shower with an inch or so of very hot water and let it soak loose the glue for half an hour or so. In most cases, if these decals are not too old, they can then be pried away with a dull knife.

Another method for loosening these decals is to use your blow drier. With the drier on high, hold it to the side of the decal just long enough for the glue to loosen. You should then be able to peel off the applique.

To remove adhesive and glue spots left on the tub after pulling up these decals, rub with one of the following cleaners:
>   Linseed oil
>   Lighter fluid
>   Rubbing alcohol
>   Waterless hand cleaner
>   Laundry spot remover

Stainless steel sinks

These are pretty durable, but they can become spotted from water or rust. They also can be scratched. To clean safely, use baking soda as a scouring powder. It removes spots and leaves a shiny finish.

Baby oil will clean stainless steel sinks and leave a clean, sweet smell as well.

To disinfect while you clean, wash the sink with rubbing alcohol.

Tile

To clean mildew and stains from bathroom tile, particularly from the grout between tiles, apply one of the following cleaners and scrub with a toothbrush or nailbrush. After using any of these cleaners, rinse thoroughly.
>   Toothpaste
>   Vinegar
>   Chlorine bleach
>   Hydrogen peroxide

Spray oven cleaner will also remove stains from between tiles, but use caution. Spray on and let it stand for *only a few seconds.* Wipe off, rinse *very* thoroughly, and repeat with another short application and thoroughly rinsing if necessary. Do not leave this on your tile for longer than a few seconds.

If your bathroom tile really needs a face-lift or you want to change the color, some but not all tiles cover well with expoxy paint. If you want to try this, you might test paint a spare tile or one in a hidden spot. Follow directions that come with the paint exactly (especially for the drying period).

Denture adhesives can be used as emergency glue for loose tiles. They are formulated to withstand moisture, a problem with ordinary household cements and glues in steamy bathrooms and kitchens.

Toilet bowls   Blue water rings in the bathroom bowl can be erased with a pumice bar, available at hardware stores.

To remove rust stains from toilet bowls, rub with a paste of hydrogen peroxide and cream of tartar. Rub in with an old toothbrush and then thoroughly rinse away the paste.

To make cleaning the toilet much easier, pour a bucket of water in the bowl before you start. This will cause the water to flush out, but the bowl will not fill up again. You can scrub away on the empty bowl.

Most toilet-bowl brush holders are inefficient little gadgets at best—flat on the bottom and open on one side. Put the drippy brush in the holder and the water will usually run out onto the floor. Solve this problem by setting a small plastic margarine container inside the holder to catch the drips. Neat, easy and absolutely free.

Cupboards, Cabinets and Counters

Clean laminated plastic cupboard doors and countertops with spray, liquid or paste wax that cleans as it polishes.

General cleaning

Enameled metal cabinets should be washed with window cleaner or automobile cleaner, then waxed with automobile wax.

Discoloration on countertops can be removed with baking soda and a damp sponge.

Clean unglazed ceramic counters with an ammoniated cleaner or ammonia and water. Leave on for about five minutes and then scrub with a nylon scrubber. After cleaning, you might want to use a permanent clear sealer to keep dirt and grease out and ease future cleaning. Most paint stores sell a clear acrylic that can be brushed or sprayed on the tile.

For painted wood cabinets, wash with a solution of 1 cup sudsing ammonia, ½ cup vinegar and ¼ cup washing soda in 1 gallon of water. Rinse with clear water.

For wood cabinets coated with varnish or shellac, make a solution of 3 tablespoons linseed oil, 1 tablespoon turpentine and 1 quart of hot water. Mix well and let cool. Use this to wash a small area at a time and then dry thoroughly with a dry cloth before proceeding to the next area. For a final finish, polish with any good liquid furniture polish or wax.

To preserve an unfinished wood butcher-block style counter, clean after each use with hot soapy water or bleach to disinfect. Rinse well. After *each* such washing, rub in a thin coat of mineral oil. Rub the oil in well and wipe off any excess with a clean dry cloth.

Burn marks

Burn or scorch marks on wood counter tops can sometimes be bleached out with ammonia. Apply carefully with an eye dropper so that only the burned area is treated. If this doesn't work, sand lightly with fine steel wool or sandpaper. Wash thoroughly after using either of these techniques to be sure all fine particles are removed. Touch up the sanded area with varnish or shellac if your counter is so finished, and polish with furniture polish.

To remove heavy adhesive-backed paper from walls, drawers, counters or shelves, try running a bit of hot water just on one corner of the paper. This may loosen it enough so that the corner can be grasped and the paper peeled away. **Removing adhesive-backed shelf paper**

For more stubborn adhesives, set your blow drier on hot, and direct the air flow at a corner edge. As the glue softens and the corner loosens, pull the paper back, keeping the hot air directed at the surface on which you are working so that the glue under each bit is softened as you peel away.

Another method for loosening these papers: Cover the shelf with a cloth and then iron with a hot iron. Do not use steam and do not iron directly on the paper without using a cloth. This should loosen the glue all over so the paper can be peeled away.

Major Appliances

To clean a discolored enamel interior, put ½ cup of bleach in the empty machine, then run it through the regular washing cycle. **Dishwashers**

To keep your disposal fresh, clean and in good working order, let the disposal run for about fifteen seconds after you think everything has been ground up. Then let the cold water **Garbage disposals** run another fifteen seconds after turning off the disposal. This keeps the disposal clean and prevents clogged pipes.

To deodorize your disposal, run citrus peels—lemon, orange, grapefruit—through it.

Ranges and ovens   Of course, commercial oven cleaners are generally very effective and fairly easy to use. But in between major cleanings, ammonia is an inexpensive method for removing light soil and for spot cleaning. For allover cleaning, leave a container of ammonia in the oven overnight. This should loosen the grease and grime enough so that it can be washed away easily the next day.

Apply ammonia to fresh spills, let stand a few minutes, and wipe away with a damp soapy cloth.

Ovens with glass doors frequently carry instructions to avoid using commercial oven cleaner on the glass. That, of course, does not stop them from getting dirty anyway! To remove brown grease stains from such doors, make a paste of baking soda and a little water, spread over the surface and let it stand for a few minutes. Then just rinse and polish.

When cleaning a built-in oven that has cabinets below it, protect those cabinets from drips. Fold several sheets of newspaper over the open cabinet doors, close the doors to hold the papers in place, creating a drop cloth canopy. As each sheet gets soaked, tear it off and there's a fresh one in place.

Oven racks

This is sometimes the hardest part of oven cleaning. These pointers also work for the grills of outdoor barbecue grills.

Spray the racks with oven cleaner right in place as you do the rest of the oven. After the specified cleaning time for the product you're using, take the racks outside and rinse off with the garden hose. The pressure of the water removes most of the grease and dirt and there is no worry about splashing the floor or cabinets with cleaner. If the racks are not entirely clean, give them another spray of the cleaner right out of doors, let dry and then rinse off again with the hose.

Remove the racks from the oven before cleaning and place them inside a large trash bag. Put paper towels between and over the racks in the bag and saturate with ammonia. Quickly close the bag, tie securely and let the bag stand overnight or several hours. Then rinse, using the hose method described above if convenient.

Another way to use this ammonia-in-the-bag method is to put the racks in the trash bag, then just pour 1 to 1½ cups of ammonia into the bag. Close it up tightly and tip the bag back and forth to spread the ammonia around.

Self-cleaning and continuous-cleaning ovens

Never clean these ovens with conventional oven cleaners. The chemicals in such cleaners can severely damage the special interior finish. Although the self-cleaning style oven (one that has a special cleaning cycle) is less susceptible to damage than the continuous-cleaning style, if a highly caustic commercial cleaner is not completely wiped away, use of the self-cleaning cycle on prolonged high heat could promote even more aggressive action on the part of any cleaner residue than that which it normally causes, thus damaging the porcelain enamel surface.

If a self-cleaning oven does not clean itself satisfactorily, the cycle may be set for too short a period of time and should be lengthened. You may also not be using the self-cleaning cycle frequently enough. For maximum effectiveness, thoroughly wipe out the oven interior with a damp cloth before using the self-cleaning cycle. Excess grease and spillovers need to be removed to avoid overloading the smoke eliminator.

Microwave ovens   Although food rarely bakes onto the interior of a microwave oven so that it cannot be simply wiped away with a damp cloth, most homemakers have learned that there is no such thing as the impossible. If this problem should happen to you, put a cup of water onto the oven, let it come to a boil and leave it in the oven for about a minute. The steam should loosen the food spill enough so that it can be wiped away with a paper towel.

To deodorize the interior of a microwave oven, wash the cold oven with 1 quart of warm water to which you have added 4 tablespoons baking soda. Wipe with a clean damp cloth.

Range burners

To keep unused burners clean and grease-free while cooking, cover them with aluminum pie plates or pot lids. This is especially useful when you're frying or cooking something that tends to spatter.

Enameled burners on a gas stove can be scoured with a soap-filled steel wool pad.

Boil cast-iron burners in a pot full of water to which you've added ¾ cup washing soda (use an enamel pan). Then rinse and dry thoroughly.

To remove heavy, burned-on food and grease from burners and drip pans, place them in an air-tight container, add a cup of ammonia (or enough to cover) and then seal. Leave them in the ammonia overnight and they should wash clean easily.

Refrigerators and freezers

For a streak-free shine on enamel refrigerators, freezers and other appliances, wipe with undiluted rubbing alcohol.

Stainless steel appliances are prone to streaking. Clean free of grease, fingerprints and any soil with baby oil on a soft cloth, then wash with club soda and finally buff with a dry cloth. Never use steel wool or abrasive cleaner on these surfaces.

Remove stickers and decals from refrigerator doors by taping a cloth wet with hot water and white vinegar over the stickers. After half an hour or so, the edges of the stickers should loosen. Remove them with a quick, hard jerk.

Tape and adhesive marks (after the tape has been pulled off) can be removed by spraying with hair spray and wiping off.

After washing chrome appliances, give them an added luster by polishing with waxed paper. An empty bread wrapper will do if you want an absolutely "free" shine.

Refrigerator gaskets can harden and crack from the use of detergents and cleansers, destroying the seal needed for energy-efficient operation. Clean gaskets with a mild vinegar and water solution. Then rub with a very light application of petroleum jelly.

For a handy, nondamaging scoop to clean frost and melting ice out of your freezer during defrosting, use a dustpan with a rubber tip on the rim.

Small Appliances

Coffee makers   To clean coffee and water stains from electric percolators and the water chambers of electric drip machines, fill the pot or chamber with cold water and add 2 tablespoons of a water conditioner (softener). For a percolator, replace the basket and stem, put on the lid, plug in and let it run through entire perking cycle. For a drip machine, cover water chamber, put pot in place and again, let it run through the regular cycle.

Instead of water conditioner, you may also use the above method using 2 teaspoons of cream of tarter or 1 tablespoon automatic dishwasher detergent.

If you don't have a bottle brush that will fit through the tube section of your percolator, saturate a small cotton ball with dishwasher detergent and push it through the tube with a knitting needle. Repeat several times.

Electric frying pans and corn poppers

Burned oil or grease is a problem with these appliances. To remove, sprinkle baking soda over the burned oil, let it stand for ten minutes, rub with a damp sponge, rinse and dry. Baking soda emulsifies grease as it cleans.

Electric can openers

Run a paper towel through the cutting mechanism as though you were opening a can. The towel will absorb the grease and grime.

For a more thorough cleaning, spray wheels and cutters with alcohol. Wipe with a damp cloth or sponge.

Irons

To clean a clogged steam iron, pour vinegar and water (half and half) into the water chamber, turn to "steam" and leave iron on for five minutes or so. Be sure the iron is sitting on a thick pad of newspapers to catch any sediment that may steam out. Unplug and let stand until vinegar solution cools, empty, and any loose particles should come out with the water. Wipe iron with a damp cloth.

To remove starch from your iron, rub beeswax or candle wax over the cool, disconnected iron to soften the starch. Then wash with a mild scouring powder on a damp cloth or sponge. Rinse off with a cloth wrung out of clear water and dry thoroughly. Be careful not to get any water into the electrical connections. When iron is dry and clean, turn it on to warm and rub over a piece of waxed paper so it will glide smoothly.

Melted plastic

This is a not uncommon, and very annoying, problem with irons, toasters, countertop ovens and any other heat-producing appliance. To remove it, reheat the appliance, and when plastic is warm wipe it off with a paper towel saturated with vinegar. Any residue can be rubbed away with a soap-filled steel wool pad (if it will not harm the finish) or a nylon net scrubber (not plastic if the appliance is still warm!). Rubbing alcohol will also remove the residue.

Another method is to reheat the appliance and then pour a small amount of cooking oil on it. Wipe off immediately with a paper towel, then wipe all oil residue away with a wet cloth or sponge.

Waffle irons

Waffles will not stick and burn to a properly seasoned iron. To season yours, first be sure all burned food and grease are thoroughly cleaned off. Unless yours has a nonstick coating, a stiff wire brush or steel wool pad can help in cleaning out all the grids. Then season by applying melted fat or oil with a pastry brush, making sure every surface on the grids is covered. Close, turn on low heat and leave on for eight to ten minutes. Then wipe off any excess fat.

Pots and Pans

Aluminum

To remove brown stains common in aluminum pans, boil water in them to which has been added 1 or 2 teaspoons of cream of tartar. These stains can also be removed by cooking tomatoes or some other acid food in them. Clean such stains from the outside of the pan with tomato catsup and a fine steel wool pad.

To prevent aluminum pans from turning black while boiling eggs in them, put a tablespoon of white vinegar for every two eggs in with the water.

Burned-on, baked-on food

Dog owners who hate to clean messy broiler pans might like this clever pointer. To clean a broiler pan which has been used for any kind of meat, put a small amount of clean water in the pan, and let it simmer for a few minutes on a low flame. This will loosen the cooked-on grease and the resulting broth of meat juices makes a nice stock to pour over your dog's dry food.

Ten Ways to Remove Burned-On Food

1. Fill the pot with hot water and add 2 tablespoons baking soda. Let soak ten to fifteen minutes, then wash as usual.

2. Sprinkle baking soda on the spots and scrub with a moist sponge.

3. Fill pot with hot water and add 2 teaspoons cream of tartar. Simmer on the stove for a few minutes, then wash as usual.

4. Two teaspoons of automatic dishwasher powder can be added to the pot along with enough water to cover the burned spot. Let soak until food loosens.

5. Soak overnight in hot water and a powdered household cleaner. The next morning, scrape burned particles with a rubber spatula. Wash as usual in soapy water and use a steel wool pad or nylon scrubber (depending upon the finish on the pan) to remove any remaining stains.

6. Take the pan outside and lay it upside down in the grass. Leave it overnight and in the morning (thanks to the dew) the pan can be easily washed clean.

7. Use aluminum foil crumpled into a ball as a heavy-duty scrubber.

8. Rub with sand and a damp cloth. This is very useful while camping.

9. Scorched enamel pans can be cleaned by adding a small amount of liquid bleach to the panful of water. Let it soak overnight before cleaning.

10. Sticky (although not necessarily burned-on) foods like baked beans or scalloped potatoes that are difficult to clean out should be put in the refrigerator overnight. The cold softens what sticks to the sides of the pan and in the morning it will scrape clean very easily.

Clean and recondition old cast-iron skillets or pots with the **Cast iron** following method:

1. Heavy grease accumulation on cast iron can most easily be burned off. Do this outdoors; an outdoor grill, fireplace or small campfire in a safe place would all work. Put the pan right into the fire and just let the grease burn off. If you have a self-cleaning oven, you can use it to clean such a pan at the same time you self-clean the oven.

2. Rust spots and other dirt will have to be scoured off. You can do this with scouring powder and steel wool or a stiff brush. Wash thoroughly.

3. Before the pan can be used, it must be reconditioned. Spread a generous layer of vegetable oil or unsalted fat all over the inside of the pot or skillet and cover. Put in a warm oven for several hours, rubbing the fat around in the pan every half hour or so while it seasons. When this is done and the pan has cooled, wash thoroughly with *clear* hot water (no soap) and dry well.

4. For the next several times that the pan is used, rub a thin film of fat around the inside after it has been washed and dried. Eventually, the only care your pan will need is thorough washing with hot water after each use. Do not wash with soap or detergent since that will remove the seasoning. A stiff brush can be used for removing food particles. Always be sure to dry the pan thoroughly to prevent rust.

Copper

To remove tarnish from copper pans and utensils, sprinkle a thin coating of undiluted vinegar over the tarnish, then apply an even coat of table salt. The tarnish can then be rubbed away with a dry cloth and the pan rinsed with hot water.

Tomato juice or catsup is also an excellent copper cleaner.

Enamel

This material also can turn brown when cooking certain foods. Enamel is best cleaned with a soap-filled steel wool pad.

Teakettles

Here are some handy remedies for cleaning your teakettle of that heavy mineral sediment.

Boil 2 teaspoons of cream of tarter in a quart of water in the kettle for a few minutes, then rinse thoroughly. A few clean pebbles can be added while it's boiling to help break up any thick deposits.

Boil a mixture of white vinegar and water in the kettle, then scrub away any sediment with a soap-filled steel wool pad.

Set the empty kettle outside on a cold night, or put it into the refrigerator or freezer. Leave it overnight. In the morning, put the kettle on the stove for just a few minutes, rinse in cold water and the deposits will rinse out as well. Shake the kettle while rinsing to help loosen any tough sediment.

To clean out brown stains from a tempered ceramic type tea-pot, scrub the inside well with lemon juice and salt.

More Kitchen Clean-ups

Coffee stains on plastic

To remove coffee and tea stains from plastic cups, soak them in a solution of baking soda and water. Or wet a damp cloth with vinegar, dip it in salt and then rub.

Foaming denture cleaning tablets are very effective in removing stains from plastic. They're also very good at removing stains from the insides of vacuum bottles.

Dishwashing drainers and trays

Soak water sediment off in water and bleach. Or sprinkle with baking soda, leave it on for three or four days, then easily wash both soda and sediment away. To keep these items easier to clean, spray with furniture wax or polish.

If you have a dishwasher, you can keep your pot scrubbers, dish cloths and bottle brushes always fresh and clean by storing them in the top rack of your dishwasher. They'll be freshly washed automatically every time you do a load of dishes.

Egg yolk

Plates covered in sticky egg yolk will clean more easily if you let them soak in cold water until ready to wash.

Foil pans

When cleaning aluminum foil pans to be reused, use a toothbrush to get crumbs and food particles out of those tiny crevices.

Pastry boards

An easy way to remove dough stuck to the board after kneading bread or rolling pastry or cookies is to sprinkle salt on the board, then rub with a damp cloth.

Sticky plastic ware

Flexible plastic bowls, pitchers, etc. frequently acquire a sticky feeling with time. To remove it, rub baking soda on the plastic with a moist paper towel. Then wash in soapy water.

Another remedy for that stickiness is to rub the pieces thoroughly with shortening. Again wash in hot soapy water to finish.

And here's a final tip useful for all those other pointers that use baking soda to clean, shine and brighten. Keep a supply of baking soda in a clean empty spice box with a shaker top. It's much easier to handle than the usual cardboard box and you can just shake what you need on all those pots, pans and countertops whenever they need that little cleaning boost.

CHAPTER 7

Small Treasures: Cleaning China, Silver, Objets D'Art

These are the items you're most likely to worry about when they need to be cleaned—fine china, glassware, silver, jewelry, small decorative pieces made out of unusual materials—all the little things that can make life such a joy, and cleaning time such a headache. These pointers will help you keep these treasures fresh and new-looking with a minimum of effort.

Alabaster

Alabaster should not be washed, but rubbed with a bit of petroleum jelly or a soft white wax.

Artificial flowers

Plastic flowers can be washed by gently dipping up and down in sudsy water until clean, then rinsed and allowed to air dry away from heat. They can be brightened and slightly shined by spraying with hair spray after drying.

Dust *beaded* flowers with a soft brush. To wash, again dip up and down in mild suds and rinse. Blot dry with a soft cloth and lay in a warm spot, such as a sunny window, to hasten complete drying so the wires will not rust.

Silk flowers should be placed in a large paper bag (such as a grocery bag) to which you've added a cup or two of table salt. Close the bag and shake gently for a couple of minutes. When flowers are removed from the bag, shake salt off carefully.

Books

When you dust books, wipe the leaf edges away from the binding to keep the dirt out of the binding.

To remove damp and mildew from books, first dry them by spreading the pages of the book and fanning the volume in the air, or placing it in front of an electric fan. Sprinkle cornstarch or talcum powder between the leaves to absorb more moisture, then brush off after a few hours. Brush mold away at the same time.

Brass

You can made a good brass cleaner at home by mixing a paste of lemon juice and salt. Some people add a tiny bit of flour to bind it together. Rub brass with this paste and the finest steel wool pad you can get. Then wash thoroughly in hot water and suds.

An even older recipe for brass cleaner is to mix a paste of lemon juice and stove ashes (wood ashes). You can also rub vigorously with a ball of crumpled aluminum foil rather than steel wool.

If your entire brass piece does not need to be cleaned, but you want to remove tiny green spots, rub spots with a piece of lemon rind dipped in salt.

Candle holders   Clean wax from candle holders easily out of doors. Place them on a newspaper, pour boiling water over them and they'll come clean as a whistle without wax pouring down the sink drain.

To remove burned-down votive candles from their cups, place the cup and candle in the freezer overnight. Next morning a tap on the bottom will make the wax fall out intact and the cup can be washed like any other glass.

Another method for removing these candles, or for cleaning wax off any nonmetal candleholder, is to put the holder upside down on a paper plate in your microwave oven for about two minutes on high. The glass will not heat up so you can immediately wipe all the wax out with a paper towel.

China   For really shiny china, wash in hot sudsy water as usual, but rinse in cold water. Budget bonus: saves on hot water!

Aluminum and stainless steel can leave black marks on highly glazed china. To remove, rub toothpaste on the mark with a paper towel. This erases the mark magically!

To clean delicate china vases or pitchers of sediments and stains, crumble egg shells into the vase, add water and shake well. This is safer than the popcorn or pebble method described under glassware, since china is more easily chipped or scratched.

Vinegar added to the water when cleaning china will help dissolve sediment and dirt.

Crystal chandeliers

These can be cleaned fairly easily with a solution of vinegar or ammonia water, or electric dishwasher detergent and water, or alcohol and water, and rubbed with a soft cloth. To speed up the job when your chandelier is made up of many small prisms (a tedious job to wipe them all) fill a tumbler with vinegar and water or an alcohol and water solution, and raise the tumbler so each pendant or drop is immersed in turn. Allow to drip-dry. Parts that are not accessible to the tumbler can be wiped off with a rag soaked in the cleaning solution. This method leaves no water spots, lint or finger prints. Be sure that the area under the chandelier is well protected.

Games and toys

Playing cards can be cleaned with a dough-type wallpaper cleaner. Or dampen a soft cloth, dip it in baking soda and wipe each side of each card. After cleaning either way, sprinkle talcum powder on the cards and shuffle a couple of times to restore that slick feeling.

Stuffed animals that cannot be washed can be cleaned with carpet cleaner. Rub on, let dry overnight and brush with an old hairbrush.

If the outer fabric of the stuffed toy is washable, but the stuffing is not, clean with mild soapsuds and a soft brush. Take care not to let water soak into the stuffing. Use the same method for rinsing. Let air dry or toss in the drier on an "air fluff" (no heat) setting.

If you want to convert such stuffed toys with nonwashable stuffing into those with washable stuffing, open a seam, remove stuffing and refill with shredded foam. For future cleanings, just toss in the washer.

Long-haired stuffed animals can be sprinkled with a mixture of half cornmeal, half salt. Leave it on for a while, then brush out.

Glassware   Hard water or a greasy sort of film can cause cloudy glasses. To remove this film, wash thoroughly, then add a few drops of ammonia to the rinse water.

A small amount of borax or a teaspoon of cornstarch in the rinse water when washing crystal and glassware will make it sparkle.

Hard water stains can be removed from glass by rubbing with a soft cloth and vinegar and salt.

To clean cloudy decanters and bottles, roll up small pieces of soft brown blotting paper, wet them and put them into the decanter. Pour in a small quantity of powdered soap, dishwasher detergent or liquid soap and fill about three-fourths full of warm water. Then shake well. Rinse in cold water. Wipe the outside and turn upside down to drain.

To remove old water rings from the inside of glasses, fill a slightly larger container with warm water to which you've added some tea leaves. Turn the glass upside down in this and let it stand for a few hours. Wash in hot suds, rinse in hot water. If stains remain, follow the same procedure using a strong solution of hot vinegar.

Polish cut glass by dipping it in a container of water with the juice of one lemon added. Dry and polish with a soft cloth.

Foaming denture cleaner will clean tough stains such as those left in flower vases. Use as you would on dentures, then rub with a soft cloth or brush.

To clean small-necked bottles of dried food particles, heavy mineral sediments, etc., fill with hot water, vinegar and a handful of unpopped popping corn or small clean pebbles. Shake vigorously. The popcorn is great at loosening tough deposits.

Tea-stained glassware can be cleaned and kept sparkling by mixing your favorite dish detergent half and half with vinegar.

When glasses have been stacked and are stuck together, fill the top or inside glass with cold water, then set the lower or outside glass in hot water. They will come apart with practically no danger of breakage.

Ivory

Ivory yellows naturally with age. However, you can maintain its original whiteness a bit longer by cleaning occasionally with a weak hydrogen peroxide solution. For regular cleaning, dust and wipe gently with a sponge moistened in sudsy water. Rubbing with a piece of lemon dipped in salt may also help preserve whiteness. Wipe off with a soft damp cloth.

Jewelry

To clean jewelry, place it in a small dish, cover with half ammonia and half hot water, and let soak about an hour. It will then need only a gentle brushing with a soft brush (an old toothbrush is good). Let dry on a paper towel.

To prevent jewelry from tarnishing, coat with clear nail polish.

Oil paintings

If dusting with a soft brush does not effectively remove dust from oil paintings, blot with a piece of soft fresh bread.

Potted plants

Use a soft brush to dust plant leaves, particularly those of the big-leaved plants that really collect dust.

Give your plants a shower. Either mist to remove dust or place under your own shower (strong, large-leaved plants only, please) for an allover wash.

Keep leaves glossy and clean by rubbing gently with a little salad oil on a facial tissue.

Removing price stickers

When you've bought any of these delightful treasures for your home or a gift, the thrill can be ruined if you can't get the price sticker off. Here are four time-tested methods for removing sticky stickers.

1. Spray with hair spray and rub off.

2. Remove glue residue with lighter fluid.

3. Rub on peanut butter with a finger, then wash the item as usual.

4. Laundry prewash spot removers also work wonders for removing the glue residue from these labels. They also remove stickiness left by tape on windows, cabinets, refrigerators, etc.

Seashells

Recently collected seashells that have a strong, offensive odor may still have the animal in the shell. To clean out inhabited shells, put them in a bucket and cover them with boiling water. Leave overnight and the next day you can insert a screwdriver in the end and pull the innards out, leaving the shell clean. Wash with detergent water, then clear water. Drip-dry.

A novel and perhaps easier way to clean such shells is to bury them open side down in an anthill for six to twelve weeks. Ants will carry out the flesh without spoiling the delicate color or finish of the shell. When the shell is clean, wash in suds (soak if necessary) and then rinse in strong vinegar water to complete the cleaning. Do not leave shells buried during freezing weather.

Silver

If you run out of silver polish, a little baking soda on a damp sponge will work just as well.

An excellent emergency silver cleaner, particularly for silver jewelry, quick touch-ups, or while traveling, is toothpaste. Just rub on and rinse. An old toothbrush is also useful for this.

Clean powder puffs are excellent for cleaning and polishing silver. There is no danger of inadvertently scratching a piece.

Mexican silversmiths keep their silver gleaming with a paste of baking soda and lemon juice. Rinse in hot water and dry carefully.

To remove extremely heavy tarnish, try this quick-soak method. Place silver on aluminum foil lining an *enamel* pan, add boiling water and 4 teaspoons of baking soda, let stand for a bit, rinse well and rub to a shine with a soft cloth. Do not use for pieces with cemented-on handles.

CHAPTER 8

Banishing Odors

Household Odors

Air fresheners

An old-fashioned rose jar makes a pretty, long-lasting freshener for your living room or bedroom. Pull rose petals from the flowers when they are starting to open and are full of fragrance. Lay in a box in shallow layers so they do not mildew, then put in a warm, dry place to dry naturally. When completely dry, simply pack in a pretty glass jar with a lid. When you lift the cover, the lovely fragrance of roses will fill the room.

Sprinkle a bit of cologne on light bulbs (when cool and turned off, please). When the lights are on, the heat from the bulb will activate the cologne and scent the entire room.

Burning scented candles is another good way to deodorize a room. These are very effective in eliminating the odor of cigarette smoke.

Dampness and odors in basements can be eliminated by placing small bowls or paper cups of baking soda around the perimeter of the room. Each week loosen the soda by stirring and replace the soda with a fresh supply every three weeks if necessary.

Another remedy for damp, musty rooms is cat litter. Sprinkle on floors and leave for a few days, then sweep or vacuum up. Or place open boxes or trays filled with litter about the room.

Remove stale odors by pouring a little clear ammonia in a shallow dish and let it sit out overnight. In the morning, odors will be gone.

As a last resort for removing severe household odors, you can burn newspaper. Put a small piece (¼ to ½ of a sheet at a time) in a metal container, put the container in the center of the room away from curtains or anything that could catch on fire, and light the paper in the container. Use with extreme care, of course, but this can be very effective when all else fails.

Books

Dry out mildewed books by airing in the sun or in front of a fan, then sprinkle French chalk or cornstarch between the pages to complete the drying process. Then, to remove any remaining odors, place each book in a plastic bag, add some whole cloves, seal the bag and leave for two or three weeks until the mildew odor had disappeared.

Bedding

Place an old nylon stocking stuffed with cedar shavings or flat pine boughs between a mattress and box spring to disguise musty odors.

Place fabric softener sheets between mattress and box spring and on top of the mattress before putting the pad and bottom sheet on. This is also helpful for pillows. Place a fabric softener sheet on the pillow before covering with the pillowcase.

Sponge smelly matresses with a strong vinegar and water solution, then dry and air in the sun. Be careful not to soak mattress stuffing.

For strong urine odors on mattresses that have soaked into the mattress stuffing, cut a hole in the ticking around the problem area. Remove the affected filling and restuff with foam rubber, clean rags, old nylon stockings, etc. Patch with a piece of sturdy fabric.

Carpets and rugs

Carpets pick up all kinds of odors: cigarette smoke, pet odors, spilled food and just plain dirt. Pick one of the following solutions for *your* carpet odor problem.

Dog and cat urine can be very stubborn odors, and if not removed, they'll attract pets to use the same spot over and over again. To remove, sponge fresh stains with club soda. If any odor remains, apply rubbing alcohol with a terry towel. Other remedies for pet odors and other carpet odors:

Sponge with a solution of white vinegar and water.

Cover area with a layer of table salt at least one-half inch thick. Leave on a day or two (you might cover this with an upside down box so it's not disturbed), then vacuum up. Be sure to empty the vacuum immediately afterward and wipe off the parts that have come in contact with the salt. It can corrode your vacuum.

Sprinkle generously with baking soda, leave it on for several days and vacuum as you would with the salt treatment described above.

Sprinkle rug with ground cloves, then vacuum. This is particularly nice in the kitchen where a spicy aroma is appropriate.

Closed containers

Remove musty odors from closed containers or the food odors left in jars and containers you want to use for other things in any of the following ways.

Fill dry container with crumpled fresh newspaper and/or charcoal. Seal and leave for twenty-four hours, then wash in hot sudsy water.

Wash with baking soda on a damp sponge or a paste of soda and water.

Place open jars and containers in the sunshine outdoors for several days.

Rinse container, then add a few drops of vanilla and water, swish around and rinse again.

After washing containers which you will be storing closed for some time, put one or two paper towels in each before closing them up. The towels will absorb moisture so that the containers will remain free of any musty smell.

Fill jar or container with clean garden soil for several days. This remedy is especially good for removing the odors of sour milk or mold.

Cooking odors

To cut down on the fishy smell when frying fish, rub fish with a little mayonnaise before coating with cornmeal or flour.

If you do have a fishy aroma left in the house after cooking fish, boil a pan of water to which you've added 2 teaspoons cinnamon until the fish smell is gone. Use the pan you've cooked the fish in and that pan will be odor free as well.

Other remedies for removing the fish odor from pans: Wash pan in vinegar or leftover tea.

To prevent odors caused by cooking sauerkraut, cabbage or other strong vegetables, place celery leaves or stalks on top of the vegetable while cooking. A slice of fresh white bread placed on top of the vegetables will also absorb the steam and odor.

After using your garlic press, make it smell fresh and clean again by pressing a piece of lemon pulp through it.

Food odors on hands

To remove the odor of onions, fish, garlic or any strong food from your hands, rub your hands with one of the following:

Dry or prepared mustard
Salt
Baking soda
Toothpaste
Hot water, then cold water
Lemon juice

Furniture

To remove odors from vinyl furniture, sprinkle baking soda on a damp sponge, rub the vinyl surface, then wipe off with a clean, moist sponge.

Place small bowls or saucers of activated charcoal under sofas, chairs, etc. Small bowls of vinegar are also helpful.

A commercial carpet freshener can also be used on upholstered furniture. Sprinkle on, then vacuum off.

A couple of mothballs placed under sofa cushions will remove the smell of cigarette smoke from the sofa.

Garbage disposals   If you have a persistent bad odor coming out of your garbage disposal, thoroughly clean the underside of the rubber "fingers" just inside the drain. It's surprising how much waste can cling to these parts, causing odors.

Other odor eaters for your garbage disposal: Put cut-up lemons through the disposal. Pour a cup of baking soda down the disposal, then flush with a cup of boiling water. If you keep an open box of soda in your refrigerator, every time you change it, pour the old box down the disposal.

Fresh mint leaves put through the disposal will keep it minty-fresh.

Paint odors   Add 2 tablespoons of vanilla to each gallon of paint (less in smaller cans) and stir in thoroughly. Eliminates paint odor even in freshly painted closed rooms.

If you haven't added vanilla to your paint, don't worry; you're not stuck with the odor. A tablespoon of ammonia added to a large pail of water and allowed to stand in the freshly painted room for an hour or so will help dispel the odor.

Placing wet coffee grounds on any cabinet or closet shelves will also clear up paint odors from the room.

Put crumpled newspaper around a newly painted chair to rid it of paint odor.

When storing leftover paint, add 3 or 4 drops of wintergreen oil to each can to keep it fresh and sweet smelling.

Refrigerators and freezers

You went away for two weeks, turned the refrigerator off and left the door closed. Now how do you get rid of that terrible smell? And how about that spoiled canteloupe that you threw away weeks ago, but the odor lingers on? Here are eight ways to rid your refrigerator or freezer from all manner of odors and keep your precious fresh food smelling like ... fresh food!

1. Wash with a solution of half vinegar and half water.

2. Wipe inner surface with vanilla extract. You can also pour a little extract in a saucer, soak a sponge or cloth in it, and leave in the refrigerator or freezer overnight.

3. When you're going to be away and want to leave the refrigerator or freezer turned off during that time, defrost thoroughly, then leave ½ cup of ground coffee in it, and close the door. When you return, the nice fresh smell of coffee will soon disappear and there will be no lingering musty smell.

4. Wash with warm water and baking soda.

5. Keep an open box of baking soda in your refrigerator. Replace every two months.

6. Wash freezer or refrigerator with tincture of green soap.

7. Place open containers of activated charcoal in the freezer or refrigerator. A good source for this is a pet store; it's used for filtering the water in tropical aquariums.

8. Wash the box with lemon juice.

Trunks, closets and drawers

Odors in closets, particularly in storage places like basements, are frequently caused by dampness. To eliminate both the dampness and the odor, make bags of a strong lightweight material (old cotton pillowcases and sheets, T-shirts or lingerie are all good materials) and fill them with commercial cat litter. Sew them shut, then place the bags on the closet floor and shelf. Occasionally hang the litter-filled bags in the sun to dry out, then put right back in the closet or storage room.

Odors in drawers, trunks, handbags, etc., can be removed by crumpling fresh newspapers into the enclosure. Close up and leave for a couple of weeks.

If you like the smell of turpentine, it makes a great deoderizer for trunks. Just place a small open bowl of turpentine in the trunk, close it up and in a few days musty odors will disappear.

Place fabric softener sheets in drawers and closets for a sweet clean smell.

Keep an unwrapped bar of soap in drawers and suitcases to prevent odors.

To prevent the odor a cedar chest imparts to clothing, shellac or varnish the inside of the chest. To restore the cedar aroma (which repels moths), sand the interior with coarse sandpaper, then follow with fine sandpaper.

Instead of lining your dresser drawers with plain paper, spray tissue paper with your favorite perfume, let it dry overnight and then use to line your drawers. An extra bonus: the light scent on your clothes will allow you to cut down on the amount of perfume you normally use.

Wipe the inside of musty drawers or trunks with a cotton ball soaked in vanilla.

Place two or three pieces of charcoal in a pint jar and stand the jar on the closet shelf during damp weather to prevent musty odors.

Sprinkle whole cloves, stick cinnamon or whole vanilla beans in drawers to keep contents fresh and sweet.

Laundry Odors

1. Soak washable clothes in a solution made with 3 tablespoons salt in a quart of water for an hour or so, then wash.

Seven ways to banish perspiration odors

2. Sponge underarm stains with colorless mouthwash.

3. Add ⅓ cup baking soda to wash cycle. For really stubborn odors, make a paste of baking soda and water, apply to the problem area, let dry, then brush out.

4. Sponge stain with rubbing alcohol.

5. Pour on white vinegar, rub it in gently, then launder.

6. Dampen the problem area, rub with a bar of deodorant soap, then let the garment sit for a few minutes before washing.

7. Saturate underarm areas, collars, etc. with undiluted hair shampoo. Let the shampoo work for about half an hour, then launder as usual.

Musty odors

Clothes and linens that have been stored a long time or improperly stored frequently develop a musty odor. The following pointers are for removing and preventing this problem.

Put the garment in a tightly closed box along with a couple of opened boxes of baking soda for a week or two.

Tie cedar shavings up in an old nylon stocking. This can be hung in a closet, closed up with clothing in a box or left in drawers.

Cologne and perfume aromas linger in the bottles long after the actual perfume is gone. Put open empty bottles in your drawers—particularly nice in your lingerie drawer.

To remove the smell of mothballs, put clothes, blankets or linens in the clothes drier with a fabric softener sheet and a damp washcloth. Five or ten minutes should do it.

Leather goods—coats, handbags, shoes, etc.—can be loosely wrapped in clean tissue, then packed in a box or drawer surrounded by lots of crumpled newspaper. Close up tightly for a couple of weeks to remove odors.

Household linens will also have a fresh spicy scent if you sprinkle a few whole cloves or pieces of stick cinnamon in your linen drawer or closet.

Loosely wrap pieces of charcoal in clean tissue and scatter them in storage drawers or boxes.

Shoe and boot odors

Remove odors from boots, shoes or slippers by wiping the insides only with a cotton ball soaked in rubbing alcohol.

To dry out and remove odors from wet shoes or boots, stuff them with crumpled newspapers. Let them air dry naturally away from stoves or radiators.

To keep children's sneakers (or your own!) smelling sweet, cut your own inner soles from fabric softener sheets, using the shoe sole or the child's foot as a pattern. Fit them inside the shoe and replace every couple of weeks. Softener sheets that you've already used in the drier once are fine and a good way to save money.

_____

CHAPTER 9

Pest Control: Getting Rid of Bugs, Mice, and Other Pests

You don't have to share your home with uninvited guests—the insect and animal variety, that is. Nor do you have to spend a fortune on professional exterminators. These home remedies for ridding your house of ants, roaches, mice, moths and all the other annoying pests that regularly invade human habitations are effective and many of them are far safer than strong commercial repellents and insecticides.

Insects

Ants

All of the following are effective ant repellents. Select the procedure that is most appropriate for your particular ant infestation.

Place cucumber skins in cabinets and under and behind the sink and large appliances. When skins are completely dried out, replace with fresh cucumber skins.

Sprinkle ground cinnamon along ant trails.

Fill an empty pump spray bottle with white vinegar. Spray along ant trails and under appliances.

Mint leaves scattered through cabinets will not only repel ants, but will give off a fresh clean aroma as well.

Sprinkle borax powder along trails and around any entrances where you think ants may be getting into the house.

If you can track ants down to where they are coming into the house, draw a heavy chalk line around their entranceway. Many ants refuse to cross this chalk line.

Sprinkle coffee grounds all around the outside of the foundation of your house. This will prevent ants from coming in.

If you can track ants to their nest, destroy them by pouring boiling water or an ammonia and water solution (1 part ammonia to 3 parts water) into the nest or anthill. A plastic squeeze bottle is good for this because it forces fluid into the hole of the hill.

The easiest way to catch ants crawling on the floor or counter is to blot them up with masking tape. With a little pressure the ants stick to the tape.

Crickets

To rid your home of crickets, blow fresh pyrethrum powder (available at many garden nurseries and hardware stores) into any places where you think they hide. Try using a bulb-style meat baster to blow the powder into cracks and holes, but be careful. This powder is poison and must be kept away from pets, children, food stuffs and off your hands.

If crickets in the house are keeping you awake at night, you can stop their chirping by making the room *completely* dark. Be sure all lights (even small nightlights) are off, and shades and drapes are pulled to keep out any outside light.

Fleas

Fleas can be a real problem in some parts of the country. To rid a room of a mild infestation, spray the room thoroughly with an insecticide for flying insects. Close off the room for an hour or two. Repeat in two to three days.

To get fleas out of a carpet, sprinkle moth flakes all over the carpet and leave them there until they evaporate.

Flying insects

Keep a can of hair spray handy whenever you're working in an area where you're likely to be bothered by bees, wasps or other flying insects. A squirt of hair spray immobilizes their wings and works faster than many commercial sprays.

To keep flies from coming in a door that is being constantly opened and closed, cut a long plastic garbage bag into strips up to about six inches from the top. Tack this across the top of the door. Whenever the door is opened and closed, the plastic strips billow out like a curtain, chasing the flies away from the doorway.

Troublesome bees and wasps can ruin picnics and make your yardwork almost impossible. Pour a little pancake syrup (the cheapest brand you can find) into old bottles or jars, and place the bottles in unused areas of the yard to attract the pests. Very effective and absolutely safe.

To keep wasps out of your garage, soak strips of cloth in household disinfectant and hang them on either side of the garage door from the rafters, and around any other likely entranceways.

Garden pests

Onion sets placed in the garden or in pots near house plants will repel aphids.

Coffee grounds placed around plants will keep away spiders and other bugs and will also fertilize and aerate the soil.

Moths

An old nylon stocking can be turned into a number of moth crystal bags to hang in closets and place in trunks and drawers. Pour 1 cup moth crystals into the stocking, then tie two knots, pour in another cup and tie two knots, and so on until the entire stocking has been used. Then cut between each set of two knots. Bend hairpins to make hooks for easy hanging.

If you don't like the smell of mothballs or crystals, whole cloves scattered in drawers or placed into nylon bags will repel moths with a more pleasant scent.

Cedar chips can also be used to make fresh-smelling moth repellent bags.

Roaches and water bugs

The most effective substances for getting rid of these persistent pests are borax powder and boric acid. Sprinkle one or the other under and behind the sink, appliances and cabinets, around plumbing and around any holes or cracks where they might be coming into your house or apartment. These powders can also be mixed with a little powdered sugar, then placed in small trays or jar lids to attract and kill roaches and water bugs.

Silverfish

Sprinkle epsom salts in empty suitcases, under drawer lining paper, in closets and along baseboards to get rid of and prevent silverfish. The remedies for roaches are also effective for silverfish.

Spiders

To rid a room of an infestation of spiders, clean away all webs using a broom covered with a clean cloth. Be sure to crush any egg sacs and burn all trash accumulated from sweeping down cobwebs. After surfaces are thoroughly clean, spray well with a good household insecticide, being sure to spray all corners, cracks and crevices. Close off the room for about an hour to allow the insecticide to work.

After you've cleaned them out, keep spiders out of the house with moth crystals. Place the crystals in small mesh bags and tape them at intervals of about three feet across the tops of the outside of the windows. When the crystals evaporate, refill the bags.

Weevils

These are those nasty little bugs that appear from nowhere in flour, cornmeal, cereals and other grain products and dry staples. To prevent them, drop a couple of bay leaves into canisters or boxes containing any of these foods. The leaves will give off a slight aroma, but will not appreciably affect the flavor of the product. You can also tape a couple of leaves to the inside of the lid of the canister, or place them in a small cheesecloth bag before dropping into the flour or meal.

If you've had a problem with weevils, they may be hiding in shelves and in cupboards ready to invade fresh supplies even after you've thrown away the infested flour or cereal. Get rid of them by sprinkling coarse ground black pepper on shelves and under liner paper in drawers and cupboards.

Another way to prevent weevils: Freeze all dry food (rice, flour, cake mixes, cereals, etc.) solidly for three hours. This will kill all eggs and larvae commonly found in such products. Freeze all new supplies immediately after shopping. If you already have an infestation, freeze everything in the cupboard, even if a product shows no visible signs of bugs. Weevils can hide in the seams of boxes and packages of all kinds of food.

Mice, Rats and Other Creatures

To keep mice and rats from coming into your house, search out all cracks and holes where they might enter. Stuff these openings tightly with steel wool. Moth balls placed around these openings will also repel mice.

Good bait for mouse and rat traps: peanut butter, fried bacon, oil-packed sardines, salami.

If you can't stand the thought of picking up a mouse trap with a dead mouse in it (and they are unsanitary), place the baited trap on a large square of plastic wrap. When you've caught the pest, simply pick up the four corners of the wrap and toss the entire package away.

Another method for disposal of mouse and trap: Place the baited trap in a wastebasket tipped on its side. After the animal is trapped, the basket can just be picked up and emptied into the trash. Such a basket is easy to wash and disinfect afterwards, too.

To keep raccoons and rabbits from destroying your crop of sweet corn, plant the corn in the middle of a bean patch. The tangled vines of the bean plants will discourage these animals long before they reach the corn. **Garden raiders**

Keep birds out of fruit and nut trees by hanging inexpensive metal wind chimes in the trees. You'll find the glitter and music enchanting, but the birds will stay away from your precious fruit. Aluminum pie pans can be used to make your own chimes.

Puppies love to chew anything they can sink their teeth into. Either red pepper or oil of cloves sprinkled on anything you do not want used as a doggy teething ring will discourage most pups. **When pets become pests**

To keep neighborhood dogs from using your yard or garden as their personal "restroom," plant oregano in any areas they habitually use. You might want to plant it especially around trees and bushes since dogs find these spots attractive and dog urine and feces are harmful to plants.

A mothball or two in the garbage can will usually keep out dogs, raccoons, skunks and other night marauders, as will a sprinkling of ammonia.

To keep cats from walking, sleeping or scratching where they are not wanted, sprinkle area with black pepper, curry powder or vinegar. Wet towels spread on such surfaces as vinyl car roofs, lawn furniture, etc. will also repel them.

PART II

Repair It

CHAPTER 10

Clothing Repair

Clothing prices are zooming upward. Who can afford to replace an entire wardrobe every year at today's prices? You won't have to, if you follow these pointers. Here's first aid for clothing for the entire family—minor alterations, repairs and ways to get longer life out of items you *thought* you were going to throw away.

Buttons

Sew loose buttons on with dental floss. It's much stronger than ordinary thread and will last much longer.

To keep buttons on longer, put a dab of clear nail polish over the threads in the center of each button.

Here's an easy technique for making fabric-covered buttons. Use standard button forms designed for making fabric-covered buttons. After cutting the fabric to the size of the pattern on the button card, hand sew a line of stitching all around the edge of the fabric, leaving the end of the thread loose. Put the button in the center of the fabric and draw up the end of the thread so that the fabric gathers up around the button form, push the back in and the button will be covered without wrinkles.

Before cutting buttonholes, mark each place with clear nail polish and let it dry. When you cut through this, you'll have straight, nonfraying edges.

Coats and jackets worn around the edges

Frequently, perfectly good coats and jackets will become worn around the edges where they button and on collars and cuffs. But that's no reason to throw them out. Buy a contrasting or matching colored heavy duty seam binding or bias tape and use it to bind all around the outside edges of the coat— around the collar, up the front opening, around the hems of sleeves, even around the bottom hem if it is complementary to the style of the coat. Be sure to take the coat along when you buy the tape so you can choose the most complementary color.

Drawstrings

Drawstrings will slip into casings easily if you put them in the freezer for a while first. The frozen string will slip right into the casing without difficulty.

Use long hair clips when putting up a hem to avoid unsightly pin holes in the fabric.

To remove iron-on hemming tape, place an iron (set at the same temperature used to apply the tape) on the tape and leave it there for a minute. (Do not let the iron rest on the fabric of the skirt itself. You may have to mask the fabric with towels or pressing cloths placed above and below the tape line.) This should soften the adhesive enough so that the tape can be pulled away while it is still warm. This can be a painstaking process, but if removing the tape means saving an otherwise unusable item, it's certainly worth a try.

When lengthening hems, remove the crease line left by previous hemming with white vinegar. Wring a clean cloth out of white vinegar and use this cloth as a pressing cloth over the crease.

A too-short shirtwaist dress can be worn under a skirt as you would a blouse. It won't come untucked like ordinary blouses and serves as a slip as well.

To remove pilling from knits, shave them! Those extra-safe disposable razors have blades set in such a way so that you can carefully shave off the fuzz and pills from sweaters without damaging the basic yarn.

Knits

Snags and pulled threads in knit garments are a common problem. Here are two tricks for corralling those pulled threads into the inside of the garment, after which the snag will be far less noticeable.

Push the little wire loop of a needle threader from the underside of the fabric up through the middle of the snag. Put the snagged thread through the loop and pull it to the back.

Push the snagged thread back through the garment with an ordinary round toothpick, using a gentle rolling motion. Push near the base of the pulled thread. If it is a long thread, push a portion of it through and then turn the garment to the wrong side and work the rest of the thread through by gently pulling it with your fingers. Any puckers or dimples can usually be smoothed away.

Slightly snug acrylic knits can be stretched to fit. Moisten with steam, then block to desired size by pinning to a towel-covered board or the ironing board until dry.

Knit cuffs
Knit cuffs often wear out before the jacket they're on does, especially on children's jackets. There are a number of ways you can replace them. Here are three easy and inexpensive ways.

Cut the cuffs off an old worn or too-small sweater. Or look at rummage sales where you may be able to buy old sweaters for as little 25¢ or so. Cut the old cuffs off the jacket, cut the "new" cuffs off the sweater, and then sew them on the jacket.

It's easiest to baste the cuffs on by hand first, then sew securely by machine. The rest of the sweater that supplied the new cuffs can also be unravelled, and the yarn used for other knitting or crocheting projects.

Athletic or other heavy socks have ribbed tops which make excellent replacement cuffs. You may even have old socks in which the feet have worn out, but the tops are still good. Measure the appropriate length for the cuff, then stitch around just above where you are planning to cut to avoid ravelling, then cut and stitch onto the jacket where the old cuffs were removed. This is also a good way to lengthen the sleeves of children's jackets.

If you knit, you can very easily make your own cuffs. Use the old ones as a pattern. Simply knit two, purl two, for the rib pattern until they are the desired length. Sew the side seam and sew onto the jacket by stretching the cuff to fit around the sleeve.

Pockets

When replacing worn pockets in winter jackets or coats, make the new pockets out of heavy flannel for a warmer pocket.

You'll feel safer carrying large amounts of money or credit cards if you sew a small, flapped pocket inside each coat or jacket. Use Velcro or some other fabric closure material on the flap and you'll have a very secure little pouch to safely carry any valuables.

Repair holes in pockets with a patch of iron-on adhesive fabric rather than trying to darn or sew them. To keep the adhesive from adhering to the wrong fabric if the hole is large, place aluminum foil under the layer of fabric being patched.

Rips and tears

Expensive down jackets, nylon windbreakers, raincoats, or suede jackets may all occasionally get minor rips or tears in them. To make an almost invisible repair at home, use adhesive iron-on tape. Place the article carefully on your ironing board so the edges of the tear just meet. Apply a piece of the iron-on tape over the tear (to the wrong side of the garment), cover with a pressing cloth and press according to directions on the tape package. Be sure to press so that the tape is well sealed to the fabric, especially around the edges.

Shoes and boots

To take the squeak out of leather shoes, pierce a few tiny holes in the shoe sole where the shoe starts to arch or curve slightly, just in back of the ball of the foot.

Replace shoelaces with lengths of narrow elastic. Turns your Oxfords into slip-ons. This is especially convenient for handicapped or elderly people who may have difficulty tying laces, and for small children.

If shoelace tips have raveled, dip the ends in white glue.

Many shoes have an elastic band under the tongue, which can be too tight and cause aching feet. To relieve this problem, either clip the elastic in one or two places (just an eighth of an inch to allow the elastic to stretch farther) or poke several holes in the elastic with an awl or large darning needle.

When the stitching around moccasin-type loafers comes un-sewn, resew it with a large needle and dental floss. Dye the floss with a felt-tipped marker.

To give winter boots and shoes a nonskid sole, cover the bottom of the sole with white glue, then press it down into a box of sand. Let dry. One treatment will last all winter.

For nonslip sling heel straps, glue a piece of moleskin (available where footcare products are sold), or flat elastic into each heel strap. Either material will keep the straps from slipping down your heels.

If you crochet house slippers, cover the soles with iron-on adhesive tape. The slippers will wear much longer and the iron-on fabric is washable.

Stretch boots that are too tight in the calves by dampening the leather with rubbing alcohol, then wearing the boots for several hours. The leather should mold perfectly to your legs.

You can help toddlers learn which shoe goes on which foot by sewing "kissing buttons" on their sneakers. Sew a small button on the inner side of each shoe so the buttons face each other. The children know they've got their shoes on right when their buttons "kiss."

Sleepwear

Washable carpeting such as that used in bathrooms and for small throw rugs can be used to make nonskid soles for children's pajama feet. The nonskid backing of the carpeting is the bottom of the foot and the carpeting itself provides a cozy lining to keep little feet warm.

A hospital-style gown for a sick child is much easier to change than conventional pajamas without disturbing the child. You can make one out of men's regular pajama tops. Locate the center back of the pajama jacket, then cut from the bottom up and even through the collar if there is one. Face the cut edges with matching bias tape. Make ties of twill tape and place one pair at the neckline and another pair a few inches below. Button up the front, then sew the lapped edges together on the sewing machine. This is also great for adult patients.

Snaps

When snaps no longer stay closed, put a small square of paper over the bottom half of the snap, then close. The extra thickness of the paper will make the snap hold.

Socks and hose

Pantyhose that have run above the knee can be turned into knee-highs to wear under slacks. Cut hose just above the knees. Then remove the waistband elastic to use as leg bands. Measure around each calf just below the knee for the correct length of bands. Snip the elastic where it is comfortable and sew the ends together to make the leg bands. Turn the edge over once on the stocking piece to prevent running and attach the elastic band by using the zigzag stitch on your sewing machine.

Elastic waistbands from discarded pantyhose can also be used to replace stretched-out elastic in the tops of socks.

A dab of petroleum jelly will stop a run, as will a dab of clear nail polish.

If knee socks are too tight, stretch them over a roll of paper towels after washing.

The color can be restored to faded pantyhose by dyeing with coffee. The coffee must be very strong and hot and the hose must be completely damp. Any dry spots may not come out the same color as the rest of the hose. Put hose in the coffee bath to soak for half an hour or so. For a deeper color, you can boil them for several minutes. While the hose are in the dye bath, stir frequently to avoid streaking. The wet stockings should be a shade or two deeper than what you want; they will get lighter as they dry.

Tight collars

If a shirt collar is slightly too tight, try ironing it cross-wise. Start in the middle and iron outward in both directions, stretching the fabric slightly as you go.

Another remedy for too-tight collars is to sew the top buttons as close to the edge of the neck band as possible, using elastic thread. The give in the elastic thread makes the neckband seem much larger.

Worn knees

When the knees in children's jeans or pants become worn, remove the back pockets of the pants to make matching patches.

To prevent knees from wearing out before the rest of the pants, iron on adhesive knee patches to the *inside* of new pants. The knees will last at least as long as the rest of the jeans or pants.

Zippers

Lubricate a sticky zipper by rubbing well with candle wax, paraffin, a bar of soap or an ordinary pencil lead.

To shorten a zipper that is too long for the garment you want to use it in, always cut it off from the top rather than the bottom. Put closed zipper in as usual, then open to the bottom, cut off the excess at the top and sew across the top tapes, or tuck under the facing of the garment and stitch across a couple of times.

To keep zippers working smoothly after laundering, always keep zippers closed while washing.

CHAPTER 11

Maintaining the Outside of Your House and Garden

You've cleaned and fixed up the inside of your home, now what about the outside? Maintaining your house and yard in tip-top condition can be hard work, but we've got some pointers that will make some of those chores easier. You'll also find some automobile pointers and a few tips on maintaining your backyard recreational equipment like the children's swimming pool and the barbecue grill.

Doors, Windows and Screens

Doors Take the squeak out of hinges by spraying with a nonstick coating used in cooking.

Another quick treatment for squeaky hinges is to spray with furniture polish.

Wash aluminum storm doors (and aluminum window frames) with soap and water, then rub on a bit of lemon oil with a cloth. Mineral oil also works. If the doors are very dirty and have started to rust, clean with naval jelly.

To sand a door that jams at the top or bottom, glue rough sandpaper in place where the door sticks. Open and close the door repeatedly and it will sand itself to a perfect fit.

Windows   Want to wash second-story windows safely without using a ladder? Nail a sponge onto the end of a long pole, soak it well with soapy water and wash away. To rinse, use your garden hose.

In cold weather, use windshield-washer solution to wash your windows. It contains anti-freeze and will not freeze and streak the windows.

For easy sliding windows and screens, wax the tracks with car wax, silicone spray or bar soap. This is also excellent for sliding glass doors.

Screens   Here's a quick, work-saving way to wash all your window screens in one easy session. Lay screens flat on the ground. Using a broom and a bucket of hot sudsy water (if screens are very dirty, add 1 or 2 cups of vinegar), sweep across the screens first in one direction, then the other. Turn them over to do the other side. Rinse with the garden hose and prop them against a wall or fence to drain dry. If you're doing this in preparation for winter storage, stack them when dry and cover with an old sheet of plastic.

Waxing window screens before putting them up will keep them clean longer. Dust will not cling so easily to the waxed surface.

Porch, Patio and Driveway

Before repainting a cement porch or stairs, remove old paint with a wire brush and wash with a ten- to twenty-percent muratic acid solution to remove dirt and grime. (Wear rubber gloves and handle the acid solution with care.) Muratic acid is available in paint and hardware stores.

Cement and concrete

To remove rust stains on concrete, sprinkle dry powdered cement on the stains, then rub with a piece of sandstone until the stains are gone.

1. To remove old oil stains, spread trisodium phosphate on the stains, then sprinkle on just enough water to dampen the powder. Leave on for an hour or so, then scrub with a stiff brush. Rinse well with a hose.

Five ways to remove oil stains from your driveway

2. Pour kerosene on oil spots, scrub lightly with a steel brush, then rinse thoroughly with the hose.

3. Pour charcoal lighter fluid on the oil stain, let it sit, then rinse off with the hose.

4. To remove fresh oil spills, sprinkle heavily with cat litter, cornstarch or sawdust. Allow the material to thoroughly absorb the oil, then sweep up and rinse away any remaining residue.

5. Spray oil stains with a laundry spot remover, allow it to sit for a few minutes, then scrub off and rinse.

Iron railings

To renew rusty iron railings and prevent them from rusting further, paint them first with an oil-base aluminum paint, let them dry and then paint with the preferred color of enamel.

Weed control

Boiling salty water will prevent grass and weeds from growing between stones, bricks or sidewalk slabs. Dissolve 1 pound of salt in a gallon of hot water, then pour this solution in any cracks or spaces where weeds are likely to grow.

Sprinkle borax between the stones in early spring to prevent weeds from sprouting.

Snow removal

To make snow shoveling easier, spray the shovel with furniture polish or a nonstick coating used in cooking. Snow will slide off the shovel easily.

For even easier snow removal, don't shovel, sweep! Use a push broom to clean snow off your walk and patio, without stooping or heavy lifting.

Place a large sheet of heavy plastic next to a pile of raked leaves, rake the pile onto the plastic, then just pull the plastic sheet to your compost pile or trash bin. The sheet can also be picked up by all four corners and easily carried. **Leaf raking**

Backyard "Toys"

Before using your grill, spray it with a nonstick coating used in cooking to make clean-up chores faster. **Barbecue grills**

If you have a self-cleaning oven, you can use it to clean the outdoor grill too. Just put grills, spits and drip pans in the oven and run the self-clean cycle. Clean oven, clean barbecue.

At the beach, preclean the grill after using by rubbing it under the sand. All excess food is rubbed off and all you have to do when you get home is give it a quick wash.

To keep dirt out of the children's wading pool, place a pan of water at the edge of the pool and insist that the children step first into the pan before getting into the pool. **Pools**

You can make a handy leaf skimmer for a small pool with a wire coat hanger and an old pair of pantyhose. Cut the legs off the pantyhose and drape the panty portion over the top of the wire hanger. Tie a knot on each side where the legs have been cut off and at the top of the hanger. Use the hook of the hanger as a handle. This could also be attached to a long pole or thick piece of doweling to use on a larger pool. Either way, this skimmer does an excellent job of gathering up leaves, grass and other debris from the surface of the water.

Vinyl pools and birdbaths that have yellowed can be whitened with a solution of bleach and water. Let it stand overnight, but be sure to cover it so birds will not be harmed by the bleach.

Children's slides   After washing down the children's slide, restore its slickness by rubbing the surface with a piece of waxed paper.

Auto Tips

To remove rust from your car's chrome, rub with ordinary mud, then rinse well.

Whenever you must leave your car out in winter weather, put a piece of tape over all the door locks. The tape will prevent the locks from freezing.

If car locks are frozen, they can be easily opened by heating the car key in the flame of a cigarette lighter or match, and then inserting the key in the lock for a couple of seconds. Repeat this procedure as many times as necessary to melt the ice so that the lock can be opened without forcing it.

Keep an asphalt shingle or two in the car trunk throughout the winter. When you're stuck in the snow or ice, lay the rough side of the shingle down to provide traction for the tires. This is much easier and neater to use than sand.

CHAPTER 12

Repairing Household Furnishings and Equipment

Furniture

These pointers are for touching up minor scratches, scrapes, dents, knicks and otherwise giving a face-lift to worn, slightly damaged pieces.

Beds and bedding
If your mattress habitually slides and shifts slightly off the boxspring, place a sheet of thin foam between the two.

Remove the ends from worn fitted bed sheets and sew them on mattress covers and sheet blankets so they fit like contour sheets.

If your contour sheets split open at the corners long before the sheets are worn, insert a piece of the stretchy portion of a cotton athletic sock into the corner. It gives enough to take the strain off of the machine stitching as you stretch the corner of the sheet over the mattress. Usually doing this to only one corner will be all the sheet needs to fit better and wear longer.

To keep satin sheets from sliding off the bed, put the bottom sheet on right side up and the top sheet on wrong side up so both right sides are together.

To keep a comforter from sliding off the bed, stitch a cotton sheet blanket onto the wrong side of the comforter.

When binding on a blanket becomes worn, make a new binding with leftover scraps of material. Small prints make especially attractive bindings.

Another way to replace a blanket binding is to crochet an edge a couple of inches wide all around the edge.

If you're too tall for your bed and your feet hang off the end, you can make an extra-long sheet by sewing half of an old sheet onto the end of your regular-length sheet. Your feet may still hang off the edge of the bed, but this longer sheet will stay tucked under the mattress and your toes will stay warm.

Lampshades   Paper shades can be attractively renewed by covering them with wallpaper.

Here's an easy way to transform an old fabric lampshade: Remove the old fabric from the wire frame. Next, wrap 1¾-inch ribbon (any color, but you will need quite a few yards of it, depending on the size of the shade) vertically all around the shade. A thin line of glue can be applied around the top and bottom wires to hold the ribbon securely in place while wrapping. Trim with gold braid around the top and bottom of the covered frame. You might also trim the shade with a few strips of braid around the shade itself.

Rugs   Small throw rugs often have rubber backings which wear off after frequent washing and years of use. You can restore this nonskid feature—or add it to a rug without such a backing—in a number of ways. Try one of the following:

Simply place a rubber bath mat under the rug. Try to match the rubber mat as closely as possible in size to the rug. If you like, the bath mat can be attached to the rug with double-faced carpet tape.

The back of the rug can be painted with liquid latex (available at arts and crafts supply stores). The rug will still be washable after this treatment.

Rubber jar rings can be sewn to the corners of the rug and if the rug is large (a hallway runner, for example), at intervals along the edges.

Cut a piece of nonskid plastic runner the size of the rug and apply with double-faced carpet tape.

Upholstered furniture

To repair small simple tears (not holes) in vinyl-covered furniture, use a strong adhesive-backed tape like carpet tape. Cut a piece about two inches wide and twice as long as the tear and slip it under the tear. Then smooth the edges of the vinyl together so they just meet. Apply some pressure to be sure the tape adheres all over.

Keep sofa slipcovers in place by placing a length of old broom handle or doweling behind the cushions to weigh down the slip-cover fabric.

If your sofa is too soft and hard to rise from, place a piece of thin plywood under the cushions.

Wood

Scratches in walnut can be disguised by rubbing with a walnut meat. The scratch disappears. Scratches in other woods can be disguised with the following remedies:

Wipe scratches on dark furniture with mayonnaise.

Brown liquid shoe polish can be rubbed on scratches or chips on brown furniture. White shoe polish is good to use on white walls when you've filled a nail hole or crack.

Eyebrow pencil is another good emergency scratch hider. Its softer color can be rubbed in and blended with regular furniture polish.

Light surface burns on wood furniture can often be rubbed away with a flannel polishing cloth and your usual furniture polish. Oil of peppermint is also good for a surface burn.

For deeper burns on wood, wrap a bit of the finest steel wool around a tiny stick (a match stick or toothpick would be good) and rub the scratch, being careful not to damage the adjacent areas. Brush off the resulting residue. Apply turpentine with a bit of soft cloth and let it dry. Next apply a coat of shellac to the spot, dry and repeat until the wood is the same color as the rest of the piece. Polish as usual when completely dry.

Household Equipment—Repairing Odds and Ends

All kinds of little gadgets and sundries may need minor repairs from time to time. Browse through these pointers and you'll probably find something you can use right now.

Faded plastic flowers can be brightened and renewed with **Artificial flowers** spray paint. Use the same color as the original flowers, or try one a shade brighter. To keep the foliage clean and your hands paint-free, cut a slit in a piece of newspaper, slip the flower through the slit and pinch it shut so only the head of the flower pokes through. Spray lightly and evenly. Let dry for a few minutes and the job is done.

Glass or pottery bakeware that is slightly chipped may still **Bakeware** be usable. Smooth the rough, chipped places with fine sandpaper or an emery board. After thoroughly rinsing away any filings, the piece is safe to use again.

An infrequently used blender may not start immediately **Blender** upon turning it on. If the blades are not turning but the motor is running, you can usually solve this problem by filling the jar with hot water to completely cover the blades. It should start satisfactorily after a few moments.

Clean an old broom and renew its usefulness by dipping it in **Broom** boiling water and baking soda. Then dry it in the sun.

To straighten candles that have been bent from heat, lay **Candles** them on a paper-covered cookie sheet in the back of a lukewarm oven for about fifteen minutes. Remove from the oven and roll on a flat surface until the candles are smooth and straight.

Diaper pins

After continued use, diaper pins tend to stick. To make them slide easily again, stick the pin into a bar of soap or dip into a jar of petroleum jelly.

Envelopes

If a batch of envelopes are stuck together, put a damp cloth over the pile with the flap side up and hold a hot iron one inch above it for a few moments. Peel off one or more envelopes (however many have been loosened) and repeat until you've loosened the whole stack.

Eyeglasses

To prevent the tiny screws holding the bows to the frame of your glasses from falling out so easily, coat the screws with two coats of clear nail polish. Let dry about ten minutes before wearing the glasses.

If you've lost a screw from your glasses, you can make an emergency substitute with a wire twist tie. Strip the paper coating from the tie so that you are left with the bare thin wire. Slip the wire through the screw holes, twist tightly around and you'll have an almost invisible fastening. Be sure to bend the ends of the wire so that you can't be scratched.

Glue bottles

Put a dab of petroleum jelly on the top of the spout of your bottle of white glue before closing it. It will open easily the next time you use it and glue won't clog the hole.

You can also put a toothpick or nail in the hole to eliminate clogging.

If your glue bottle is already clogged, screw a small screw into the hole right through the clog. You can leave this in as a permanent stopper as well.

Dull plastic knitting needles can be lightly sanded with an emery board or very fine sandpaper. They can also be sharpened carefully in an ordinary pencil sharpener, but be careful not to make them too pointed. **Knitting needles**

If your power lawn mower is balky when you're trying to start it, let it sit in the sun for a while before using it. The sun will warm up the engine and make it easier to start. **Lawn mowers**

Give new life to your measuring tape by placing it between two sheets of waxed paper and pressing it with an iron. **Measuring tapes**

To make ball-point pens start writing, warm the end of the point with a match or place on a stove burner that has a lighted pilot. Be careful not to leave it too long or the plastic may start to melt. When the pen is warm, it should write fairly easily. **Pens**

Dried marking pens can be restored. Dip the marker in a *very small* amount of a commercial ink solvent (available in stationary stores). This should soften the dried ink enough to make the pen usable again.

Phonograph records

Warped phonograph records are difficult to restore, but here are two methods that work on some records, depending on how badly warped they are.

Warm the record in a lukewarm oven, then put a heavy weight on it, leaving until quite cool. Or, put the record (without warming) between two flat boards, and weigh down with about 200 pounds of weight. Leave under the weight for a couple of days.

Photographs

Photographs that have been stained by water can sometimes be restored in the following manner. Rub the photograph with petroleum jelly. Let it set for about five minutes, then buff with a facial tissue or very soft lint-free cloth.

Ping pong balls

To repair dented Ping Pong balls, drop them into boiling water for a few seconds. The dents disappear and the balls are ready to be reused.

Picture frames

An inexpensive way to stain unfinished picture frames is with paste shoe polish. Apply several coats of the polish, buffing well after each coat for a deep glossy color.

Sewing machine needles

Sharpen your sewing machine needle by placing a piece of fine sandpaper in the machine and running the needle through it.

Wood screws

To make wood screws drive in more easily, first rub the screws on a bar of soap.

PART III

Preserve It

CHAPTER 13

Keeping Food

The best way to get the most out of your food dollar is to use every bit of food you buy. With these storage hints (including some freezing and preserving tips), ways to restore food to an edible state, and neat hints for using leftovers, you may never throw good food away again.

Baked Goods

Frozen bread often becomes damp and soggy while thawing. To prevent this problem, open the bag when you take the bread from the freezer and insert a heavy paper towel. Reclose the bag and allow the bread to thaw as usual. The towel absorbs the excess moisture and the bread will be fresh and firm.

Bread and rolls

Bread will thaw more quickly if you place the closed bag in your gas oven with just the pilot light on.

A spring-type clothespin makes a quick and easy closure for the bread bag. Many people will find this more convenient than using a twist tie.

Stale bread makes excellent croutons or bread crumbs. For croutons, you can simply place the cubed bread in a pie plate and leave in a gas oven with the pilot light on for a day. In an electric oven, turn the heat on to its lowest possible setting and watch croutons carefully so they do not become overbrown. Toast gently thirty minutes or more until they are dry and lightly browned. Store in a covered jar. These will keep for many weeks.

For more flavorful croutons, cube bread and add a tablespoon or so of melted butter or margarine to every ½ to 1 cup of bread cubes. Toast gently in the oven at a very low heat thirty minutes or more until dry and lightly browned. Garlic salt, Worcestershire sauce or other seasonings can be added for zest. When thoroughly dried, store in covered jar.

Keep stale bread in a brown paper bag until it is very dry. In this way you can accumulate a quantity of bread over a period of several weeks. When you're ready to make crumbs, just roll them out with a rolling pin or pulverize in an electric blender. Keep in a tightly covered container.

If you buy seed-covered bread or rolls, you'll find that there is always a quantity of poppy or sesame seeds left in the empty bag. They're worth saving. You can even add them to your bread-crumb jar, since they make an excellent flavor addition to most recipes using crumbs.

Cakes and cookies

Small families can have their cake and eat it, too. After preparing a regular-size cake, cut it into quarters or other suitably sized portions, place each piece on a paper plate, freeze until firm, then wrap securely. Thaw and use one piece at a time, just enough for your size family.

If you don't have a cake safe or lidded pan, keep cake fresh and moist by placing a slice of fresh bread in with the cake, then wrap the whole thing with food wrap. The cake stays fresh and the bread gets stale.

A potato chip box makes a good storage container for a 13 x 9 inch sheet cake. Slip the cake inside and wrap the entire box with foil. The box keeps the icing from being disturbed and a well-wrapped package can even be frozen.

At anniversaries, parties and weddings where cake is sent home with the guests, have your caterer wrap the cake first in waxed paper, then in a napkin or cake box. The frosting will not soak through and the pieces of cake will stay fresher.

Leftover cake or cookies can be turned into crumbs to make a delicious pie shell similar to a graham cracker crust. Mix crumbs with just enough melted butter or margarine to hold them together, then press the mixture into the bottom and sides of a pie plate. Chill for two hours. This can be filled with any favorite pie or pudding mix and topped with whipped cream for an extremely easy and economical dessert.

It seems as if every time you bake cookies, at least one panful comes out burned slightly on the bottom. Don't throw them away. Just use the finest side of a 4-sided grater to gently rub the burned crumbs off the bottoms. You can easily grate away all the burned part and the cookies will be fine.

In humid weather cookies and crackers can quickly become soggy. If your oven has a pilot light, keep such products stored in the oven. They will always be crisp.

Pancakes and waffles

If you wrap leftover pancakes or waffles in foil or plastic wrap, they can be stored in the refrigerator for a day or two. Paper towels placed between each pancake will keep them from sticking together. For a quick breakfast or snack, pop one in the toaster; they taste as fresh and good as when originally made.

Your children will love leftover pancakes made into jelly rolls. (You will, too!) Just spread pancakes with jelly or jam and roll them up. Sprinkle with a little powdered sugar. Makes a great nutritious treat.

Pies

When you make pies to go in the freezer, cut an initial in the top crust of each indicating what the filling is: "A" for apple or "B" for blueberry, for example. Wrap in clear plastic wrap or plastic freezer bags and you'll know at a glance which is which.

Extra pie dough can be turned into the most wonderful treats. Roll out the dough, spread with sugar and cinnamon, then roll up like a jelly roll. Slice as you would for refrigerator cookies, then bake with the pie for about fifteen minutes. Or cut wafer cookies out of the rolled-out dough and sprinkle with sugar and cinnamon, then bake.

Dairy Products

Cheese

Cheese can be frozen. Cream cheese should be used within six weeks; hard cheese will keep successfully for a few months. Wrap any type of cheese well in aluminum foil or heavy-duty plastic freezer wrap before freezing.

When frozen hard cheeses are thawed and used immediately, they tend to be quite crumbly. Leave in the refrigerator for a couple of days after removing from the freezer for a more natural texture.

To remove mold from a block of cheese without wasting any cheese, use a potato peeler rather than a knife.

Cheese and cheese spreads that have become hard and dry can be mashed with a fork, then mixed with mayonnaise to make a delicious sandwich spread.

Eggs

Keep freshly bought and older eggs clearly identified in the egg tray by marking the older eggs with a pencil so you'll know which to use first.

Many recipes call for only egg whites or yolks. Store leftover whites each in a separate plastic sandwich bag, then place all the bags in an egg carton. They will not dry out in the plastic bags and you can use just those you need in future recipes.

Poach leftover egg yolks in water, cool them and then put them through a sieve. The cooked yolk will keep in a tightly covered container in the refrigerator for a few days and can be used as a garnish for salads, canapes and other dishes.

Milk

If you use milk only in small quantities and infrequently, freeze it in ice cube trays. One cube is about right for a cup of coffee and more can be thawed if you need a larger amount. Milk does tend to get watery after freezing, but whole milk will seem less so than skim or low-fat milk.

Ice cream

If your freezer does not keep ice cream hard, try transferring it to covered plastic bowls. It will stay much harder at a warmer temperature than in the original cardboard carton.

Fill small margarine tubs with single servings of ice cream, cover and put back in the freezer. Family members can remove an individual serving without getting the whole carton out. Ice cream will keep longer if not allowed to soften repeatedly.

Ice cream will also hold up longer if the container is wrapped in aluminum foil before being put in the freezer.

Fruits and Vegetables

General pointers

Keep a clean sponge in the vegetable bin of your refrigerator to absorb excess moisture. All vegetables and fruits will stay fresh longer.

Keep a large container in the freezer into which you put any leftover vegetables day by day. When you've accumulated a large quantity, use them to make vegetable soup.

Bananas

To retain the color and flavor of bananas, wrap them individually in foil and store in the refrigerator to use as needed.

Cabbage

To best keep a partial head of cabbage, wrap in plastic wrap, then in aluminum foil to prevent darkening.

Canned fruit

Save the juice from juice-pack canned fruits to use as poaching liquid for poached fruits, to use in making apple sauce, and to use with other ingredients in making dessert sauces.

Celery

Remove the leaves from a bunch of celery and dry them in the oven. Use to flavor soups and stews. The same can be done with parsley and the tops of green onions.

After buying celery, cut off just a stalk or two at a time as needed. It will stay fresh if kept dry and unwashed in a plastic bag closed with a twist tie.

To freeze celery, cut or dice and package in small bags—just enough to use for a usual recipe. It freezes best if lightly blanched first. Frozen celery is somewhat soft when thawed and not desirable as a raw vegetable, but it is fine for use in soups, stews and other cooked recipes.

Citrus fruit and peels

Save grapefruit and orange peels. They can be chopped and dried or frozen to use in any recipe calling for citrus peel or zest (the colored portion of the peel).

Lemons are fairly expensive and something that you may use only in tiny amounts. Too often, half or three-quarters of a lemon may be wasted and thrown away. Here are a number of ways to keep them and their juice fresh and handy for whenever you need just a touch of this important and flavorful fruit.

Cut lemons into slices, put into individual plastic sandwich bags and freeze. These are particularly handy when you want a single slice of lemon for a cup of hot tea. No need to thaw beforehand; just remove a slice from the freezer and drop into the hot liquid.

Squeeze all the juice out of one or more lemons and freeze in small plastic containers, ice cube trays or small plastic bottles.

After squeezing lemons, don't throw the rind away. Grate and dry in an oven with a pilot light or an electric oven set at the very lowest possible heat. Watch carefully to avoid burning.

Fresh grated rind can also be frozen. If you make many recipes calling for both rind and juice, mix the appropriate proportions of the two before freezing.

When you use just a little juice from a lemon, the remainder can be kept in the refrigerator for the next use if you use the following technique. Pierce the lemon with a fork to squeeze out just the right amount of juice instead of cutting it. Then store the lemon in a plastic bag. You can also pierce the lemon with a toothpick in several places, then leave toothpicks in the holes as plugs to prevent the juice from drying out while storing.

Lemons will stay fresh for some time in the refrigerator if they are kept in a water-filled airtight jar.

Lemons that have hardened from long standing can be freshened by putting them in boiling water to cover and letting them stand for a few moments.

Garlic and onions   To prevent garlic from molding, rewrap the bud with the dry peelings after removing the desired number of cloves. Store in an uncovered container at room temperature.

Peel an entire bud of garlic at one time, then freeze the peeled cloves in a small jar or plastic container. When frozen, the cloves slice and chop easily without odor.

Keep cut onions in the refrigerator by wrapping in plastic wrap and then in aluminum foil. They will keep for a week or two without giving off an odor.

Onions can also be kept in the refrigerator in a jar with a lid on it to prevent the odor from contaminating other foods.

Chop a quantity of onions at one time and freeze in small recipe-sized portions in plastic bags. You'll always have chopped onion handy without any work or mess.

When onions start to sprout, they will keep longer if you peel them and store in the refrigerator or freezer.

A handy bag for hanging onions in your storeroom or basement can be made from an old pair of pantyhose. Put one onion into each leg and tie a knot above it. Put another onion in on top of the first knot, then tie another knot. Continue on like this until all the onions have been tied into the hose. This is easy to hang in a cool dry spot and the air can circulate through the nylon hose to keep the onions dry. When you need one, simply cut below the knot over the bottom onion and the others remain "bagged."

Green peppers

Prices vary widely on these seasonal vegetables. Buy a quantity when they're plentiful and inexpensive, wash and chop them, freeze on cookie sheets until firm. Then bag in plastic for use all year round. Frozen green peppers will not be crisp when thawed, but they are excellent in cooked dishes.

Lettuce

To keep lettuce from turning brown and soft quickly, wrap in paper towels before placing in a plastic bag. This is especially important if you've washed the lettuce before storing. The lettuce will not only stay fresh longer, but will be crisper too.

Nuts

Nuts in shells will stay fresh for a very long time if you pack them in layers of sand and store in a cool dry place. Soak them in warm water for an hour before using if you would like them to peel easily as if they had just been gathered from the tree.

To grind nuts without losing their oils in the process, freeze the nuts first and grind them while still frozen. There will be no oozing of oil and the very finely ground nuts will be light, dry and fluffy.

Chopped nuts can be kept fresh stored in plastic bags or tightly covered jars and containers for several weeks. If you use chopped nuts frequently, you'll save quite a bit of time by doing a quantity ahead, storing in this manner and using as needed.

Potatoes

If raw potatoes are starting to soften and must be cooked, you can boil them (scrub well, but don't peel), then store in the refrigerator tightly covered for a week or so. These can be peeled and slices or grated as needed for fried potatoes or hash browns.

Tomatoes

Tomatoes are the glorious bounty crop of many home gardeners. To keep a large quantity of tomatoes for future use, puree them and freeze in ice cube trays, then pop out of trays and pack in plastic bags for freezer storage. When tomato flavor is needed for soups, stews or sauces, simply use as many cubes as necessary. You can also freeze containers of stewed tomatoes or sauce.

To ripen green tomatoes, wrap in newspaper and put in a dark place. Check their progress every few days. After a few specks of red appear, the tomatoes will start to ripen more rapidly, so watch closely.

Meta

Speed up breakfast preparation by frying an entire pound **Bacon**
package of bacon at one time, drain on a paper towel and cool.
Then roll the bacon up in a clean paper towel and store in a
large tightly covered glass jar in the refrigerator. When
needed, the bacon can quickly be heated in the oven or a very
lightly greased frying pan, or used in recipes. Bacon stored
like this will keep for ten days to two weeks.

Remove frankfurters from the package and freeze sepa- **Frankfurters**
rately, wrapping in aluminum foil or heavy-duty plastic wrap.
You can use only as many as you need at one time without
thawing the entire package.

Pour leftover gravy or meat juices into ice cube trays and **Gravy**
freeze. When frozen, pop out of trays and store in plastic bags
in the freezer. These are very handy for making "instant"
gravy, or enriching soups and stews, or for use in any recipe
requiring a meat broth.

To freeze ground meat, remove from store wrapping, place **Ground meat**
in a plastic bag or wrap in foil or freezer wrap. Flatten the
meat out into a large slab before wrapping. This stores con-
veniently in the freezer since such packages can be easily
stacked, and thaws more quickly than a large mound of meat.
Label packages with type of meat, date and weight.

To freeze hamburger patties, oil a cookie sheet and then spread it with the meat. Cut through to make three-inch squares. Put the entire pan in the freezer and when frozen remove from cookie sheet with a tap on the bottom. The hamburger squares are stored in plastic bags in the freezer. This is much faster than making individual round patties and the squares fit onto conventional buns just fine.

Pork chops Store pork chops, or any meat you may want to use as individual servings, in the freezer wrapped individually. Package the individual packets together in family-size portions. The chops are ready to take out as a package for the entire family, or just one at a time for a single serving. This is great when you have family members showing up for dinner at unpredictable times.

Staples and Dry Foods

Baking powder If you've had a can of baking powder for a while, test it before using. Just pour a small amount in a saucer and add a little water. It has lost its leavening power if it does not fizz.

Canned goods If storage space is limited, make a handy cache for canned goods, flour and sugar and other dry staples by placing these foods in a large new garbage can. You can cover this with a large round table cloth and have extra workspace as well.

Breakfast cereal of almost any variety can be ground into **Cereal** crumbs in the blender and added to a favorite oatmeal cookie recipe or used to top coffee cakes, etc.

Once coffee is made, transfer to a vacuum bottle rather **Coffee** than leaving on the coffee warming plate or reheating. The coffee will stay hot for hours and retain its freshly made flavor much longer than reheated coffee.

Leftover coffee can be used in many ways. Here are just a few ideas.

Freeze in ice cube trays. Use in making iced coffee. The coffee cubes will not dilute the coffee like regular ice cubes.

Hot coffee is an excellent addition to chocolate frosting, chocolate cake or chocolate ice cream topping.

Red Eye Gravy is a tradition in the South and a wonderful way to use leftover coffee even for northerners! After frying country ham or sausage in a skillet, remove the meat and leave the drippings in the pan. Add several tablespoons of black coffee and ½ to 1 cup water. Heat the gravy, stirring constantly. Add salt to taste. This is delicious over grits and eggs, sausage or ham, and hot buscuits.

To soften hard marshmallows, put them in a wire strainer **Marshmallows** and hold over a pan of boiling water.

Marshmallows can be kept in the freezer. They thaw very quickly after which they will be soft and fresh.

Oil

Cooking oil used for deep frying can be used several times if you strain the oil after each use. An easy way to do this is to place a coffee filter in your strainer. It catches the finest sediment.

Popcorn

Opinion on whether or not popcorn should be stored in the refrigerator seems to be divided. Some say yes; others, absolutely not. Actually either way—refrigerator or cupboard shelf—is satisfactory, so long as the popcorn is in a very tightly covered container to retard moisture loss. It can also be kept in the freezer.

To restore hardened popcorn balls, close them up in a tightly sealed plastic bag with a couple of slices of fresh bread. In a day or so, the balls will be fresh and edible.

Potato chips

Stiff potato chip bags are difficult to close with the conventional twist tie. You'll find the bags close nicely if you fold the open end over once or twice, then secure with a paper clip. No more stale chips!

Stale potato chips are great when crushed and used to top casseroles or mixed into meat loaf.

In damp weather, to keep salt from sticking and clogging up the holes in the shaker, add a teaspoon of dry rice to a small-size shaker. Increase the quantity of rice for larger shakers and replace rice when refilling shakers. **Salt**

When you *think* your can of vegetable shortening is empty, there may still be at least enough left to grease a pan or two. To salvage every drop, place can in a warm oven until all bits of shortening melt, then pour out into a pan you want to grease or into a tiny container to store until needed. **Shortening**

The biggest complaint about sugar is that it gets hard. Brown sugar is usually the worst offender, but white and confectioners sugar all suffer from the same unfortunate tendency to harden when exposed to moisture or air. Try the following suggestions for solving and avoiding this problem. **Sugar**

Keep brown sugar soft by placing in a clean empty three-pound coffee can with a cotton ball taped in the inside of the lid. The cotton absorbs moisture so that the sugar does not harden.

Brown sugar also keeps fairly well in a *tightly* closed plastic bag.

A hard lump of brown sugar can be placed in a shallow baking pan and softened in a warm oven for a few minutes. This also works in a microwave oven. However, the sugar should be used immediately, since if allowed to cool, it will frequently harden again.

If you have time before you need to use the sugar, place a lettuce leaf with the sugar in a tighly closed container and the sugar will soften in a few days.

Lumps of sugar—any kind—can usually be easily grated on a standard four-sided grater.

Confectioners sugar usually does not harden as readily as white or brown. Rolling with a rolling pin is usually sufficient to break up any lumps.

Perhaps the easiest way to soften sugar is to place it in the freezer. It can be frozen container and all. After a few hours, the grains will be separate and free-running.

Tea
Instant tea and tea mixes can become lumpy. To prevent this problem, store the jar in the refrigerator after opening.

Lunchbox Pointers

To pack a piece of iced sheet cake for the lunchbox or picnic basket, cut the piece in half and place one half on top of the other sandwich style with the icing in the middle. No more icing sticking to the waxed paper or plastic wrap.

A good way to keep food cool in the lunchbox throughout the morning is to keep lunchbox treats like cake or pie in the freezer. Put the frozen pastry in the lunch pail just before you leave for work or school. The frozen food will thaw by lunchtime and will serve to cool the rest of the lunch at the same time.

Canning and Freezing Tips

Ice cubes can be removed from trays and stored in a brown paper bag in the freezer. You'll always have an ample supply of ice and the cubes don't seem to stick together in the paper bag the way they sometimes do in plastic.

When freezing foods in those bags that "zip" shut, eliminate all excess air from the bag by putting a drinking straw in one corner of the bag, sealing the bag to the straw, then sucking the air out of the bag through the straw. Remove the straw quickly and seal the tiny opening.

Save plastic cottage cheese and margarine containers with tightly fitting lids to use for freezing small quantities of leftovers. They stack well and do not break. However, these containers are not made specifically for freezer storage and are advisable for short-term storage only.

Save aluminum frozen dinner trays and use them to make your own frozen TV dinners out of leftovers. You'll be surprised how good the leftovers taste after a couple of weeks or so. Just heat foiled-covered trays in a 400-degree oven for thirty minutes or so.

To be sure frozen food stays frozen while the family is away on vacation (in the event of unexpected power shortages), store a plastic food bag filled with ice cubes in the freezer. If the cubes show signs of having melted and refrozen, you should check the condition of all foods in the freezer carefully.

To make larger, longer-lasting ice cubes, put the water in muffin tins instead of conventional ice cube trays. These larger cubes are nice to use in punch bowls or to take on camping or fishing trips in an ice chest.

Keep a list of everything you put in your freezer and how many packages of each item you have. Tape this list to the freezer so you can mark off what you use. This saves unpleasant surprises—such as when you are sure there must be one more box of strawberries in the freezer, but after searching you find there is not.

To aid in defrosting frozen food, place it on a wire cake cooling rack so the air circulates all around it. The food will thaw faster and more evenly.

An easy way to prepare jars for canning if you have a dishwasher is to wash the jars in warm soapy water, then put them all in the dishwasher and turn it on to "scald." They are all ready at one time and you can take them out one at a time to fill. This keeps the other jars hot until you need them. This process ends the mess and danger of scalding your jars in large pots of boiling water.

To make sure you have a tight seal when canning with standard canning jars, coat around the edges of the lids with paraffin.

When a canning jar is empty, clean it and put a piece of paper towel down in the jar, then another piece across the top. Screw on the metal top ring and the jar will stay clean and odor free while being stored. The ring will not rust either.

The easiest way to coat jellies with paraffin is to shave enough wax into the bottom of the empty jar so it is completely covered. Then pour in the hot jelly and the wax will melt and come to the top and cover the contents.

Here's an old-fashioned way to seal jellies and jams without paraffin. It is not officially approved by the Department of Agriculture, so if you want to try it, be sure to carefully examine all jelly for mold, change in color and off-odors before eating it.

Cut circles of wax paper or brown paper to just fit inside the jelly jar on top of the hot jelly. Dip these circles in brandy or whisky, then place on top of the jelly. Pour 2 or 3 tablespoons more liquor on top of the paper, then cover the jars with lids. People who have used this method say there is no change in the taste of the jelly from the liquor, but you must be sure to use the jelly before all of the liquor has evaporated. Check jars every three or four weeks and add additional liquor as needed to keep jelly well covered.

Cooking Disasters

The table is set, the candles are lit and your guests are ravenous—but something's gone wrong with the food. Before you send out for pizza, look over these dinner-saving pointers for ways to transform your cooking disasters into culinary delights.

Cake, fallen

If your beautiful cake falls while baking, there's nothing that can restore it to a light, airy three layer wonder, but it will still taste pretty good and you can make a delicious, even elegant, dessert from it. Just break the cake into large chunks and fold into whipped cream or prepared pudding. If you like, top with fresh fruit or chocolate sauce. You'll have an instant trifle type of dessert that your guests and family will ask for again and again.

Soggy cereal, chips or crackers can be crisped in a slow (200- to 250-degree) oven for three to five minutes.

Cereal, crackers, potato chips, soggy

Add a *tiny* pinch of salt to the pot of coffee. This should take away the bitter flavor.

Coffee, bitter and overcooked

First, chill cream, bowl and beaters thoroughly. Then, set the bowl of cream into a bowl of ice while you are whipping it. If cream still won't whip satisfactorily, add *one* of the following: 1 unbeaten egg white, 3 or 4 drops of lemon juice, a pinch of salt or a pinch of unflavored gelatin powder. This should do the trick. Incidentally, if you choose to try the gelatin, it will also stabilize the cream so that after whipping the cream will stay light and fluffy much longer. This is especially useful if you must hold the whipped cream for any length of time before serving.

Cream, won't whip

For egg whites to whip, everything—bowl and beaters—must be absolutely grease-free. Even a tiny bit of yolk in the whites will keep them from whipping. If a little yolk gets into the whites while you're separating the eggs, you can easily scoop it out with a piece of eggshell. If whites still won't whip and you've followed these precautions, try adding a pinch of baking soda to the whites.

Egg whites, won't whip

Add a couple of drops of a commercial concentrated gravy maker, or a few drops of Worcestershire sauce, or even a teaspoon of instant coffee.

Gravy, too pale

Gravy, too thin

Stir in instant potato flakes a little bit at a time until desired consistency is reached.

Gravy, too greasy

A small amount of baking soda thoroughly stirred in will absorb the grease.

Meat, underdone

If you've started carving any large piece of meat and find it is not done, finish slicing it and arrange the pieces on an oven-proof platter or pan. Put the platter of sliced meat back into the oven for five or ten minutes, checking frequently until the meat is cooked to your taste. The sliced or carved meat will cook through much more quickly than the large roast.

Rice, burned

As soon as you discover the rice has burned, turn off the flame. Then, place a slice of bread on top of the rice and cover the pot for about five minutes. The bread will absorb the scorched flavor. When removing the rice from the pot, be careful not to scrape out any of the rice that has colored or stuck to the pot. Just use the loose, unbrowned rice.

Soup or stew, too salty

Add a couple of raw potatoes, cut into chunks, to the soup or stew and let them simmer until tender. Remove the potatoes and discard. They will have absorbed the excess salt.

Add equal amounts of vinegar and sugar (a little bit at a time) to cut the too salty flavor of a soup or stew.

Vegetables, over-cooked

If vegetables of any kind are overcooked and mushy, transform them into an elegant purée. Purée the vegetables in a blender, food processor, electric mixer or by pressing through a fine sieve. Season with a little butter, cream, salt, pepper, lemon juice, herbs or whatever complements the particular vegetable you're serving. For a crowning touch, mound the purée in an oven-proof bowl, sprinkle with grated cheese and brown under the broiler for a couple of minutes.

Thicken soggy mashed potatoes, which can result from over-cooking or from adding too much liquid while mashing, by adding a little dry powdered milk. Whip in a little at a time until the desired consistency and fluffiness is reached.

Perk up not-so-fresh vegetables in one of the following ways: **Vegetables, wilted**

Sprinkle with cold water, then store in the refrigerator until serving time wrapped in a towel or paper toweling.

Blanch vegetables in hot water, then soak in ice water. A little vinegar added to the ice water will help prevent the vegetables from turning brown.

Just soak vegetables in cold water to which you've added a tablespoon of lemon juice.

The best way to store cleaned raw vegetables like celery, carrots, etc. is submerged in a jar or bowl of cold water and kept in the refrigerator. Even sweet corn (de-husked) stays fresh and sweet tasting. Parsley will last days longer than if it is stored dry.

CHAPTER 14

An Ounce of Prevention— Stopping Problems Before They Start

The best way to "solve" problems is to prevent them from happening in the first place. Wouldn't it be wonderful if every problem could be avoided by such simple measures as those suggested in this chapter! Unfortunately, these pointers won't do away with every household cleaning or repair chore, but they will show you some tricks that will make those chores easier and less frequent. You'll find ways to keep things cleaner, preserve precious treasures, keep your houseplants green and healthy—even when you go away on vacation—and some tips on keeping the family wardrobe in shape without time-consuming repairs and costly cleaning bills.

In the Kitchen

When putting away dinner plates, slip a paper napkin between each one. The napkins will protect the plates from scratches and at mealtime, simply pull out plate and napkin in one set to speed table setting.

Dishes, utensils and pans

To keep silverware from tarnishing, first clean it thoroughly, then wrap each piece separately in aluminum foil. Be sure the wrapping is tight. Place these "packages" in a plastic bag and close tightly, making sure all air is out of the bag. The silver will stay tarnish-free this way for months.

Wooden salad bowls should be protected in the same way as wooden cutting boards and butcher-block tables: Rub with mineral oil after washing the bowls. Never allow the bowl to soak in water, but wash and rinse it quickly after using, then rub again with mineral oil.

After washing wooden-handled flatware and utensils, drain them with the wooden part up. Otherwise the water can run down into the wood causing it to warp or rot.

When glass-stoppered bottles such as decanters are not being used, coat the stopper with glycerine before putting the bottle away. This will prevent the stopper from getting so tightly stuck that getting it out becomes a problem.

To protect pots and pans with nonstick coatings on them, put a paper plate in each one when not in use. Then you can safely stack these pots without fear of chipping or scratching.

Make lunch boxes last longer by lining the insides with heavy adhesive-backed paper or plastic. The box can be wiped out easily and will not rust.

Drains and plumbing

Pour ½ cup of vinegar down the sink drain once a week to help keep them open. This won't dissolve a bad clog, but regular doses could prevent one.

To keep pipes from freezing in extremely cold weather, turn on a very small drip in the bathtub from the cold water faucet. Next turn on a very small drip from the hot water faucet in the wash basin. This gives you two distinct drips (cold and hot) to check on occasionally. If either drip stops, call the plumber; but the tiny flow of water through the pipes caused by allowing the faucets to drip is frequently enough to keep the pipes from freezing. Be sure to place a sponge under the drip to prevent mineral stains in the tub or sink.

Oven and range

Keep unused burners clean while frying with spattering grease or cooking sauces that splash by covering burners with pot lids. The lids are much easier to clean than the burners.

Another way to keep the stove clean while frying is to cover the cooking pan with a colander. A "hat" of aluminum foil with steam vents cut into it works well for thick sauces like spaghetti sauce which tend to spatter while simmering.

When frying eggs, sift a little flour into the hot fat. It will keep the grease from spattering out all over the stove—and you!

When baking a casserole or anything that tends to boil over in the oven, place the casserole dish in a pan of water. Any spill-over will fall into this pan, the casserole will not burn or get too crusty on the bottom, and your oven will stay clean.

Fruit pies are notorious for boiling over and soiling the oven. To prevent this messy spill, wet a two-inch wide strip of brown paper (cut it from a grocery bag) wrap it around the pie tin, and pin the overlapping ends together securely. As the pie bakes, the paper shrinks and tightens around the pan so the juice stays in the pie. This can also help keep the edge of the crust from browning too fast.

Rubber gloves

Prolong the life of your rubber gloves by pushing a bit of cotton down in the fingertips. Both your manicure and your rubber gloves will last much longer.

Shelves

When putting adhesive-backed decorator shelf paper or plastic on kitchen shelves, allow an extra inch at each side and the back so it will come up and cover the cracks where cupboard walls join the shelf. Food particles can then be wiped off easily instead of having to dig them out of the cracks.

Soap
Bars of soap will last much longer if you unwrap new bars and let them sit on a closet shelf for a few weeks before using. Tuck the open bars among your linens and you'll add a fresh scent to them at the same time.

To keep your soap trays clean of gummy soap buildup, cut a sponge to fit in the bottom of the tray and place the soap on top of the sponge. The sponge rinses out easily and the soap stays drier and does not melt away so quickly.

Open only two holes in the top of a can of kitchen cleanser and you'll find an adequate amount shakes out but the can will last longer.

Soap pads
Cut a steel-wool soap pad into quarters before using, then use just one quarter at a time. They work just as well as a whole pad and a box of pads will last you much longer.

Store steel wool pads in a covered glass jar or covered plastic container (use a margarine or cottage cheese container). They will not rust as readily.

Rust on steel-wool pads can also be retarded by soaking them in water and baking soda before using.

String mop
After buying a new string mop, tie a single knot in each string end. The mop will last much longer and the knots help scrub the floor better.

No-Damage Decorating

You can make cut flowers last just as long as possible by **Cut flowers** using the following techniques:

Cut pulpy stem ends off at an angle with a very sharp knife. This increases the surface area through which the stem can absorb water. Every day or so, retrim the stem end.

Woody stems should be split for an inch or so from the bottom.

Remove all leaves from below the water line.

Some flowers seem to benefit from a little salt in the water. Others do well with an aspirin or two dropped in the vase. You might experiment with one or the other to see if these folk remedies work for you.

Keep flowers away from heat and sunny windows.

Storing flowers in the refrigerator at night will also keep them fresher.

Check water every day and replace it with fresh water every couple of days.

Gardenias keep well in a deep bowl (like a fish bowl) with only a little water in the bottom.

Holiday decorating   If you save ribbon bows from year to year, you can keep them from crushing in storage by stuffing each loop with crushed tissue paper.

End holiday frustration over tangled strings of Christmas tree lights with this storage pointer: After the lights have been taken off the tree, stretch and straighten them out, then gather the bulbs in groups of three or four, securing each group with masking tape. The following year, unwrap one group at a time as you put them on the tree. The string will be much easier to manage.

Painting   When sanding a wall before painting, sand with one hand and hold the open end of the vacuum hose with the other. Keep the vacuum running and use the hose to catch and suck up the sanding dust as you work to eliminate messy cleanups afterwards.

Dip paint brushes and roller pads in a mixture of fabric softener and water after washing. They'll dry as soft as new and will be much easier to use next time.

Before putting dishes or books back on newly painted shelves, sprinkle the shelves with talcum powder, then wipe off. No more sticking.

To keep couch and chairs from sliding back and marring freshly painted walls, cover wood blocks cut from two-byfours with scrap carpeting and put them on the floor between the wall and the back legs of any such pieces. The wood blocks will keep the furniture at a safe distance from the wall. If you have carpeting to match your floor carpet, the blocks will be virtually invisible.

Keep pictures hanging straight by wrapping a little adhesive tape around the hood over which you hang the picture wire. The tape will keep the wire from slipping.

Picture hanging

When hanging pictures, place a thumbtack in each lower corner on the back of the frame. The tack heads butting against the wall provide air space in back of the picture which eliminates dust marks on the wall.

Here's an inexpensive way to hang pictures *without* putting noticeable holes in the wall. Drill a 1¼-inch-deep hole with a masonry drill bit at a 45-degree angle where the ceiling and wall join. Insert one-inch plastic masonry plugs (available at hardware stores) into the holes and then screw screw eyes into these plugs. This whole assembly can be painted over with thick paint the same color as the ceiling. Paintings, plaques and wall hangings can be hung from this screw eye assembly with twenty- to-forty-pound test clear monofilament (nylon) fishing line. (Twenty-pound will handle most pictures, forty-pound should be adequate for your heaviest pieces.) The screw eye assembly is practically invisible and walls are not damaged.

Plants

You can be sure your potted plants have good drainage if you cover the hole in the bottom of the pot with a ball of un-milled sphagnum moss. An adequate substitute is a folded piece of fabric. A piece of an old sheet or terry toweling will work well.

Use a double saucer under your houseplants to prevent accidental water spots on your tables and window sills. Place the pot in a normal size saucer, then put the whole thing in a larger saucer. If you over-water and the water flows out of the inner saucer, it will be contained by the outer saucer.

You can also make "coasters" for your potted plants out of indoor/outdoor carpeting. If there is a plastic backing on the carpet, leave it on so the carpeting can be easily moved.

Protect macrame plant holders by spraying the part that holds the pot with polyurethane spray (available at paint and arts and crafts supply stores). Two or three coats will keep the macrame from rotting caused by the damp pot.

Here are three techniques for keeping your plants watered while you're away for any length of time:

1. For standing pots, put an old towel in the bottom of the bathtub and cover it with a thick wet pad of newspapers. Water the plants well and set the pots on the wet paper pad. (Remove saucers so moisture can seep up through the drainage holes.)

2. Put the pots in the bathtub (no towel or papers required) and water them thoroughly. Then stretch a piece of plastic over the top of the tub, taping it down so the plants are in an almost airtight enclosure. This will keep plants moist and fresh for two to three weeks at least.

3. Keep hanging plants watered with the wick method. Stuff the end of a funnel with cotton and insert it into the pot's soil. Then fill the funnel with water. The water will filter through the cotton slowly, keeping the soil moist.

Heavily chlorinated water can harm plants. If you must use tap water on your plants and it is chlorinated, allow the water to stand for a day before using. This will allow the chlorine gas to escape.

Small treasures

Prevent wicker baskets and decorative objects from drying and disintegrating by spraying or brushing with a coat of clear high gloss varnish.

To keep a candle straight in its holder, cut crepe paper or crisp tissue into leaf or petal shapes, arrange them over the empty holder and insert the candle into the holder over the paper so that the petals form a padding and a frame around the base. Bend the petals down by rolling over a pencil so they curl like a flower. The paper holds the candle upright and the petals catch any dripping wax.

Candles last longer and burn without dripping or smoking if they are dipped into soapsuds first. (Don't dip the wicks.) Let the candles dry thoroughly before lighting.

Candle stubs remove easily from holders if you put ½ teaspoon water in the bottom of the holder before inserting the candle.

Vases or pots holding dried flowers tend to tip over easily. Keep them upright by filling each container with gravel (aquarium gravel is handy and inexpensive) before inserting flower stems.

After cleaning artificial flowers, treat with a coat of hair spray. They'll stay glossy and beautiful and will not collect dust as quickly.

Flashlight or camera batteries will last longer if you store them in the refrigerator when not in use. However, they should be warmed to room temperature before using for maximum operating efficiency.

Children's schoolbooks can be well protected by making cloth book covers for them. Use scrap fabric in dark, dirt-concealing colors. Use the book as a pattern. A pocket can be sewn onto the outside of the cover as a handy stash for pencils or small notebooks.

Preserving Arts and Crafts

Small sculptures, snowflakes, doilies and similar items can be stiffened and preserved in any of the following ways:

Crocheted and knitted items

Dip article three or four times in paraffin. Then drain on paper toweling to remove excess wax. If items treated in this way become soiled, simply dip them in boiling water to remove wax, rinse dry and reprocess in fresh paraffin.

Snowflakes and doilies can be stiffened very satisfactorily with spray starch. Stretch and pin the snowflake to the desired shape on a piece of cardboard covered with waxed paper. Then saturate the article with spray starch and allow the item to dry thoroughly, about twenty-four hours. The article will be stiff and the waxed paper allows the excess starch to stiffen the underside at the same time.

Wallpaper paste is also useful for stiffening and preserving these items. Mix the paste to a fairly stiff consistency, then coat the crocheted or knitted item with the paste. While allowing the piece to dry, occasionally reshape it to the correct dimensions.

If you knit or crochet house slippers, you can preserve them by spraying the soles with clear acrylic paint before they are worn. Apply three or four light coats, letting each coat dry before applying the next. The yarn will wear longer and the soles will not soil so quickly.

Pictures

Hair spray is a good preservative for chalk, pastel and pencil drawings.

You can easily preserve a child's drawing or any paper picture using poster board, plastic wrap and your iron. Cut heavy poster board to the size of the drawing and place the picture on top of it. Cover the front with plastic wrap, allowing a generous excess to fold over to the back. Tape this excess to the back of the board. Cover the front with light cardboard and iron over it, using a medium-warm iron, starting from the center and working toward the corners. Apply medium pressure as you iron and be sure to work on a hard flat surface. Your picture will then be sealed and preserved. You can make a "frame" by edging it with colored tape.

Needlework Problem Solvers

Five yarn organizers

Keeping yarn or embroidery floss in order—while you're working with it and while you're storing it—can be a real headache. Pick one of these methods for instant relief. Organize your yarn with these pointers and you'll never have to face a tangled mess again.

1. Large rolls (pull skeins) of yarn can be stood on end in a small plastic wastebasket while you're working with them.

Since the yarn pulls from the center of the roll, as many rolls as will fit can be kept in the basket at the same time. You can use one or more strands simultaneously if necessary.

2. A liquor bottle carton is a handy yarn storer. They generally have twelve compartments, each perfect for stashing one pull skein of yarn for storage or while working.

3. Place each ball or skein of yarn in one of those tube-style potato chip cans, punch a hole in the plastic lid and pull the end of the yarn through the hole. The cans can be taped together into a cluster when working with multiple strands.

4. When working with multiple strands, thread each strand through a drinking straw. This keeps the yarn from tangling as you manipulate it back and forth while knitting or crocheting.

5. When rolling balls of yarn from loose skeins, roll them around the band that was wrapped around the skein. You'll always have the brand name and dye lot number handy.

Four embroidery floss organizers

1. A small plastic drawer tool box makes an excellent storage chest for embroidery floss. You can easily see the color through the clear plastic drawers and each color stays clean and untangled in its little compartment.

2. Store each color of floss in a separate envelope, marked on the outside with color and color number. These envelopes can be stored equally well in a box or your work bag.

3. Save empty thread spools and wind floss around them. A small piece of material poked into the hole of the spool makes a handy pin cushion for needles.

4. Take your supply of each color of floss and tie a string around one end. Then braid or plait the skein. Floss stays tidy and tangle-free, and a single strand can be easily pulled free without disturbing the rest.

Sewing pointers

Hand sewing is much smoother and easier if you wax your thread. Beeswax is best, but paraffin will also work. Simply draw the length of thread over the block of wax.

A small square of beeswax makes a handy pin cushion to protect needles and keep them slick and sharp.

When you have trouble threading a needle, spray the end of your thread with hair spray. This will stiffen the thread enough to make threading the needle easy and fast.

In the Dressing Room

Keep your lipstick in the refrigerator and you'll find it goes on more smoothly and feels more refreshing, too.

Beauty pointers

Storing nail polish in the refrigerator will keep it from evaporating and becoming too thick.

Your nail polish will last longer without chips, cracks and peeling if you wipe your nails with alcohol or a vinegar and water solution before applying polish.

To keep tall boots in shape while storing, hang them. Slip a metal shower curtain hook through the hole in the zipper pull. Both boots can be hung on one hook and the hook can be hung from any rod, hook or over a shoe rack.

Boots, shoes and gloves

Shoelaces will last much longer if you machine sew a line of zigzag stitching down the length of each lace. On children's shoelaces, you can sew each lace with a different color thread to aid them in telling the right from the left shoe.

Here's a pointer that will keep children's mittens and gloves from being lost in the school locker or coat closet. Sew a loop on each glove or mitten large enough to be buttoned over a coat button. Then button each mitten onto the coat. Now all you have to worry about is teaching the kids to remember to button on their mittens when they take them off!

Before putting on pantyhose, slip on a pair of sheer footlets to protect heels and toes from runs and to prolong the life of the hose.

Costume jewelry

A coat of clear nail polish will keep costume jewelry from tarnishing and turning dark.

Fabric care

Save washing instructions for large items that are not washed too often, like bedspreads, blankets or draperies, clipped to a hanger hung next to your washing machine. When you need them, the instructions are close at hand.

If you sew or knit or crochet, keep a scrap of fabric or a small worked sample to use when you want to test a cleaning method that might adversely affect the fabric. No more hunting for "an inconspicuous spot" on the garment itself.

CHAPTER 15

Storage for Long Life

What's one of the first things people look for when inspecting a new home or apartment? How much storage space it has! Kitchen cabinets, linen closets, clothes closets, basement storage areas—we can't seem to get enough of them. We all store things. These pointers will tell you how to make the most of that space, how to store clothes for a winter or a lifetime, how to save space or make new space, and how to protect your stored things. We also have some packing tips useful for storing or for traveling.

Storing Clothes

The following recommendations are for long- or short-term storage of a variety of clothing items.

Flat storage is the best storage if one has the room. Fold items as little as possible and layer them as little as possible. Should layering be necessary, put the heaviest things on the bottom.

Some items should not be hung, such as those with narrow shoulder straps, dresses heavy at the bottom such as beaded dresses of the 1920s and garments that are cut on the bias. If garments are hung they should be put on padded hangers.

For heavy clothing such as military uniforms, use wooden hangers and cover the hangers with muslin. Two wire hangers could be used together and then padded and covered with muslin. Use dust covers over clothing. Men's shirts are great for this. Never crowd items.

Group items to be stored according to color—whites vs. darks—as natural dyes can rub off. Wrap in clean white sheets or white tissue paper (not blue) but do not use plastic, newspapers or allow items to touch wood. Air out stored items at least once a year and then avoid direct sunlight. If you must use moth crystals do not .et the crystals touch the items.

Keep records of who wore the clothing and for what occasions. Photographs and other documentation can be of great value if you ever decide to donate such things to museums or university costume collections.

When packing for a long trip, pack each day's supply of **Packing** underwear or lingerie in a separate plastic bag. As needed, one set at a time can be removed without disturbing other packed articles. The emptied plastic bags will make useful laundry bags.

Wool sweaters can be packed (or stowed in dresser drawers) by rolling them to save space. Fold the sweater in half crossways, fold arms straight across, then roll. Pack rolled sweaters side by side. They are neat and take up less room. It's also easier to find the one you want than when they are stacked.

To pack a suit jacket with a minimum of wrinkling, fold in the following manner. Spread the jacket out on a flat surface so that the lining is down and the back is face up. Place the sleeves so that they line up along the back center seam. Fold the two front panels over the sleeves so the jacket is inside out. Then fold the jacket in half along the center seam, still inside out. Finally, the tail of the jacket can be folded up to make it short enough to fit in the suitcase. Folding a jacket in this way keeps the sleeves and the front as flat as possible and the few inevitable wrinkles usually come out if it is hung up as soon as it can be unpacked.

After your suitcase is packed, spread large sheets of tissue paper to cover the clothes, then top this with plastic such as a dry-cleaner's plastic bag. Tuck all the edges around the packed clothes. When baggage stands out in the rain, it is possible for water to leak into your case. The plastic will usually keep your clothes perfectly dry.

In closet and drawer

If you store items in boxes in closets, make a list of the contents of each box, number the boxes and corresponding lists and tape the lists to the inside of the closet door. You'll be able to find what you want without going through every closet and box.

Keep dresser drawers organized by using open boxes as dividers. The boxes can be covered with pretty adhesive paper and everything will stay neat.

Save drawer space and eliminate wrinkles by hanging slips in your closet. Bend up the ends of wire hangers and hook the straps over the bent-up end. White slips can be hung on one end of the hanger, colored slips on the other.

Keep children's socks neat and separated by storing in egg cartons. Each little pair fits into one section. The cartons fit nicely in any drawer.

Hang a shoe bag on the inside door of your coat closet as a catchall for mittens, gloves and knit caps.

Hide winter blankets throughout the summer by packing them in your empty suitcases—an otherwise wasted space. If you go away on vacation and need to use your luggage, the blankets can be temporarily stacked on the bed until you return.

Space Savers

In the kitchen

Make use of almost-out-of-reach top shelves and the tops of kitchen cabinets. Collect small sturdy cardboard cartons that will fit nicely on the shelf space. Near the base of each box, cut a one-by-three-inch horizontal hole that will act like a drawer pull. This makes it easy to get each box down so the contents are easily available. Box fronts can be decorated with paint or decorative adhesive paper.

Stack shoe boxes on a shelf either sideways or upended, depending on your shelf space, with the open tops of the boxes facing out. Use these boxes to store tins and boxes of spices in alphabetical order. You'll save space, keep your spices orderly and they'll be easy to find.

Attach a shoe bag on your pantry door to hold spray cans of paint, whisk brooms, dust cloths, small vacuum attachments, etc.

Inexpensive woven placemats make nice shelf liners for the china cupboard. They cushion the dishes and can be easily washed at cupboard cleaning time.

In the dressing room

A new plastic trash can makes a handy storage container for out-of-season clothes or any number of stored objects. Cover it with a flat lid or circle of plywood and top off with a pretty table cloth. You'll have a double-duty bedside table. The brightly colored cans also make ideal toy bins for the children's room. Decorate with plastic stick-ons or enamel with the child's name.

Store tiny earrings in a plastic bobbin box. Keep a small tweezers in the box to use when removing earrings from the box.

Necklaces and chokers hang neatly from a tie rack. This can be hung on the back of a closet door, or right on the wall as a functional decoration.

Keep scarves wrinkle-free by catching a corner of each in a snap-style clothespin, then hang the clothespins on a wire hanger. Several scarves can be held in each pin.

CHAPTER 16

Making Money Last: Special Budget Savers

Money—we can't tell you how to get more of it, but we can help you make what you've got go further. Here are some pointers that will help you cut down on your utility bills and some ways to make inexpensive items you already have around the house stand in for something you might otherwise have to run out and buy.

Energy Savers

Appoint a family member "Household Energy Monitor." This person is responsible for making sure all lights are turned off when not in use, all faucets are turned off tightly, the thermostat is set at an optimum energy-saving temperature and for thinking up other ways for the rest of the family to cut down on energy use. A portion of the subsequent savings on your fuel and electric bills can be awarded the "Household Energy Monitor" as a reward and incentive for a job well done. This is a great way for a school-age child to earn his or her allowance.

To save on winter heating bills, cover windows with clear, heavy plastic and seal the cracks all around the frame with tape. The same plastic can be saved from winter to winter and reused.

Cover vents on air conditioners with plastic or aluminum foil to keep winter drafts from blowing in.

If your house is heated with free-standing radiators (not backed up against the wall) cover large plywood boards with heavy aluminum foil and fasten them to the wall in back of each radiator. The heat will reflect back into the room instead of just warming up the cold walls.

If you have a window in your kitchen, you can save on air-conditioning costs by installing an exhaust fan in the window. Turn on the fan whenever you're using your oven, stove or any other heat-generating appliance. The fan will pull the heat out of the kitchen, leaving it cooler, and will pull out cooking odors as well. This is especially effective if the window is near your stove.

On hot days, keep shades and drapes drawn through the middle of the day. Rooms will stay cooler much longer.

Put lights on a dimmer-switch system. You'll only need to use energy sufficient to provide the exact amount of light you need for any particular purpose.

Instead of reheating coffee throughout the day, pour hot, freshly made coffee into a vacuum bottle every morning. It will stay hot all day. You can also store hot water in a vacuum bottle to use throughout the day for small cooking chores, preparing instant coffee and soups, brewing tea, etc.

On hot days, let the sun heat your water! Large dark-colored containers of water can be set in the sun in the morning and by evening you'll have hot water for washing, bathing, dishes, hand laundry, etc.

Small electric appliances used for small cooking chores will generally use less energy than heating up your entire oven. When you must use the oven, try to cook several things in it at once—or even the entire meal—to make maximum use of the energy used.

Invite groups of friends and neighbors over for a TV party for special TV events like major sporting events, the Academy Awards, special movies, etc. You'll have fun and save energy for your community by having only one television set turned on instead of several.

Water Savers

Keep all faucets and connections in good repair. A leak at the rate of one drop per second will waste approximately 700 gallons of water in one year.

Place a couple of bricks or a gallon plastic jug filled with water inside your toilet tank. You'll save the quantity of water displaced by the bricks or jug with every flush.

"Navy" showers save gallons of water. Turn on the water just to get wet, then turn off the water while you suds up. Turn on the water again to rinse. And a shower—unless it's a very long one—uses far less water than a regular bath.

Use a small glass of water to rinse your brush in while brushing your teeth instead of letting the water run. While shaving, run some water into the stopped-up sink for rinsing instead of letting the water run.

Save as much water while cooking as possible. When preparing something that has more than one ingredient cooked in water, try to use the same water for more than one item, either doubling up or reusing the same water. For example, when making potato salad, the potatoes can first be boiled, removed from the pot, and the eggs then hard cooked in the same water.

Water can be replaced by broth or boullion—either full strength or diluted half-and-half—for cooking vegetables, rice or noodles. The broth you drain off from these foods should be saved to make soups and sauces.

Water used for cooking can also be used for watering house-plants and gardens. Cool to lukewarm first. You'll be giving your plants some nutrients at the same time you water.

Keep a container of drinking water in the refrigerator instead of letting the tap run until the water gets cold everytime you want a drink.

Use your dishwasher or washing machine only when there is a full load. You'll save water, the fuel to heat it, and electricity or gas as well.

Always water lawns and gardens in the evening. The cool night air gives the water a chance to soak into the ground so you won't have to water quite as often. If you water in the middle of the day, water is wasted through evaporation by the sun.

Money Saving Substitutes

Newspapers torn in thin strips make a good substitute for commercial cat litter. Newsprint is a good odor controller and it's easy to dispose of. Change every day and be sure strips are not too wide.

An impromptu rack for roasting meats and poultry: Use a number of rings from canning jars.

Use a hamburger press to shape cookie dough instead of rolling and cutting it out. Place a small ball of dough between waxed paper in the press, close it with enough pressure to make the cookies as thin or thick as you like.

Christmas tree light bulbs as replacement bulbs in night lights are generally less expensive than the regular replacement bulbs.

To make a funnel when filling small salt shakers, cut the corner off an envelope.

A muffin pan makes an almost spill-proof bed tray for a sick child. Each section can hold a different food.

Using a rubber kitchen spatula simplifies spreading glue over a large surface, since it is flexible enough to spread a thin coat and stiff enough for good control.

For a convenient hot plate while traveling, take along your electric iron. Turn it upside down between two bricks. You can heat coffee or tea—even pop popcorn!

Use your garbage can lid as a work tray while weeding the garden or transplanting anything outside. You can carry your work tools on it and also have a place to drop weeds rather than having them drop on the lawn. When the chores are finished, just turn the lid over and dump into the garbage can.

An emery board makes a good fine file for the hobby kit. It works well on small wood models and miniatures.

A swivel-bladed vegetable peeler is a good substitute pencil sharpener.

Masking tape works well on disposable diapers when the tabs pull loose.

When blanching vegetables or straining food, use a large square of nylon net instead of a colander.

When making cupcakes or muffins and you do not have enough pans, use the screw-on lids from canning jars. Set these lids on a cookie sheet and put a paper cupcake liner in each one. The muffins or cupcakes hold their shape as well as when in muffin tins.

For a cheap and handy steamer, use an aluminum pie plate of a size to fit the pot used, pierce the bottom and angled sides with a sharp pointed knife at one-inch intervals and turn the pan bottom up in the pot. Makes an excellent steamer for sausages, other meats and vegetables.

A shoehorn makes an excellent small trowel to use for transplanting potted plants.

Make your own premoistened towelettes to use for baby or for removing makeup. Pull the core out of a roll of bathroom tissue and pull the last sheet up through the center. Place the roll in a large can with a plastic lid and pour baby oil over the roll of paper. Cut an X or hole in the plastic lid and push the paper end through it. You'll have a few weeks of instant wash-ups at a fraction of the cost of commercial products.

An ironing board makes an ideal cutting board for home sewers.

Cover a can of frozen orange juice with a cloth napkin or handkerchief for an instant cold compress or ice pack.

When a recipe calls for spices tied in a bag so as to be easily removed, use an aluminum tea ball.

Miniature marshmallows can be used as candleholders on a birthday cake.

PART IV

Reuse It

CHAPTER 17

Recycling

A great many things that we throw away are still good, usable items. They may not be useful for what they were originally intended, but with a little imagination, many throwaways can be turned into instant "new" gadgets for other uses. Many things you already use can also serve dual or triple purposes and other items are inexpensive substitutes for more traditional, more expensive tools. These pointers will give you all kinds of ideas to use the items you already own, or may be throwing away, in ways you never thought of. They are work savers, time savers *and* money savers.

Bottles and jars

Small pill bottles are perfect for storing sewing and handicraft items like needles, pins and sequins. In the work shop, use them for screws, nails, nuts and bolts.

Save small plastic medicine bottles (thoroughly washed, of course) to use for catsup, mustard, mayonnaise or salad dressing in packed lunches and picnics.

Improvise a travel toothbrush holder by making a hole in the plastic top of a pill bottle just large enough for the brush handle to go through. Put the top on the bottle with the handle sticking up out of the hole.

Pump-style hair spray bottles make good plant misters. Squeeze bottles such as those from dishwashing detergent are perfect drip-proof watering "cans."

Save empty shaker jars from spices and seasoning to use when dusting flour into cake pans.

A clean fingernail polish bottle is great for holding a small amount of paint saved for touching up nicks in walls or furniture. The little brush is just the right size and easy to handle and store. These bottles are also good for children's paints.

Large plastic bleach bottles and milk jugs can be used for storing and carrying all manner of things. A few uses you may not have thought of:

Cut off the tops and cut holes in the sides of such bottles to make hanging baskets for houseplants.

Cut off the tops and use the bottles to cover garden seedlings on cold nights.

Use four gallon-sized plastic jugs with caps and a towel to make a float for the children's swimming pool. Loop each corner of a large bath towel through a handle of a jug and sew in place securely. The child can paddle around the pool lying on the towel, supported by the floating jugs.

Boxes and cartons

Cereal or cracker boxes are perfect for transporting small potted plants. Use a box that is wider than the diameter of the plant and cut a hole in one side of the box so the pot can be set in the hole. The box will keep the pot from tipping over and the width of the box will protect the leaves from bumping and being damaged. It is also possible to carry more than one small plant in a large box by cutting several holes. In cold weather a piece of plastic wrap spread over the plants will protect them from exposure.

If you travel with a baby, a six- or eight-pack soda or beer-bottle carton makes a handy bottle and baby food carrier. There are no spills and it can be easily placed in a cooler to avoid spoilage.

A cardboard egg carton can be used to make quick-starting briquets for your barbeque grill. Place a charcoal briquet in each pocket and pour melted paraffin around each briquet. When the paraffin has hardened, break the pockets apart and store the treated briquets in a cool place until needed. The cardboard and paraffin light easily and no liquid charcoal starter is necessary.

Another method for making these charcoal starters is to fill the egg carton pockets with lint from your automatic drier, then fill with paraffin.

Save foam egg cartons to use as packing material when mailing or moving fragile items.

Egg cartons also make handy drawer organizers. Use in dresser drawers to hold costume jewelry, in desk drawers to keep paper clips, rubber bands and thumbtacks neatly separated.

Stuff milk cartons with shredded newspapers to use as starters for fireplaces and barbeque grills.

Plastic baskets such as those used for strawberries and cherry tomatoes make perfect storage containers for kitchen sponges and pot scrubbers. You can also crochet or macrame two or three together to make an attractive, inexpensive shower caddy to hold soap, shampoo and bath sponges.

Save plastic baskets to use as cupboard organizers. They are perfect for holding small packets of dried mixes, sauces and fruit drink powders, spice boxes and bottles and other small items.

Fill old coffee cans with a combination of sand and salt and keep a few of these in the trunk of your car for winter driving emergencies. **Cans**

A coffee can makes a good bathroom tissue dispenser for camping or other situations when a wall dispenser is inconvenient or unavailable. Cut a hole the size of a quarter in the center of the plastic lid from a two-pound coffee can. Squeeze the roll of tissue a few times until the center cardboard tube can be pulled out. Put the roll of tissue in the can and starting from the center of the roll, pull the tissue up through the hole in the lid.

Tuna fish or similar-size cans can be opened at both ends (make sure edges are smooth and not sharp) and used as egg poaching or frying rings.

Cans of various sizes with top and bottom removed make handy no-mess funnels to use when stuffing poultry. A soup can is about right for a small chicken, a large fruit can is good for a large turkey. Insert the can into the cavity as far as it will go and spoon the dressing through the can raising it as the cavity fills. Remove the can when you've used the desired amount of stuffing.

A forty-six-ounce juice can also makes a good funnel when filling pillows with foam stuffing.

Attractively decorated cans with plastic lids make perfect gift containers for cookies or baked goods.

Children can turn aluminum soda-pop cans into safe unbreakable banks. Let them decorate the cans with paper and paint. The opening in the top (which will be the coin slot) can be made safer by covering the sharp edges with tape.

Tube-style potato chip cans are perfect for storing knitting needles, crochet hooks and even a ball of yarn.

Cardboard tubes   Save the tubes from paper towels and bathroom tissue to use as mailing tubes for small items.

Cut tubes into rings with a very sharp knife or single-edge razor blade and decorate with pretty adhesive-backed paper, colored marking pens or fabric for napkin rings.

Roll freshly washed and ironed tablecloths and place mats around the cardboard tubes from gift-wrapping paper for crease-free storage.

Crayons   You can make good sturdy crayons from small broken pieces by melting the pieces in a muffin pan that has been lined with aluminum cupcake liners. When cool, you will have crayon discs that are easy for little hands to hold onto. These are also more difficult to break than regular crayons.

If you make candles, broken crayon pieces can be used to color the wax.

Fabric Softener Sheets

Those wonderful little sheets you throw in your drier to remove static and soften your clothes are wonderful for many other things, too. In fact, you can get double duty out of these little marvels by using them for one of the following ideas *after* they've done their work on the family laundry.

Eleven uses for fabric softener sheets

1. Put sheets in drawers or closets for sweet-smelling clothes and linens.

2. Clean your eyeglasses. They not only do this well, but also seem to keep glasses from fogging up so easily.

3. Polish silver.

4. Place the foam-type fabric softener sheets under the head and arm throws on furniture to keep throws from sliding off.

5. Keep a sheet in your sewing box. When hand sewing, running the threaded needle and length of thread through the sheet will slightly coat the thread with the softener to keep it from tangling.

6. Store wigs with a sheet tucked inside to keep them fresh and sweet.

7. Fabric-softener sheets make excellent dust cloths. The dust really clings to them and they do a great job of polishing.

8. Rub a sheet over your hairbrush to cut down on static electricity when brushing your hair.

9. Shine your shoes.

10. Tuck a sheet into your suitcase when traveling to keep clothes static-free and smelling fresh and sweet.

11. Fabric-softener sheets can also be used to make lovely perfumed padded hangers—for your own use, as gifts or as nice items to sell at club or church bazaars. Wrap sheets around a wood hanger and seal at the ends with white glue. Then double crochet a strip wide enough to make a case around the hanger bar. Sew on with yarn to completely cover the hanger.

Greeting cards

Cut pretty greeting cards into strips about two-and-a-half inches wide so there is a picture of some sort on each strip, make a hole near the top, run yarn through and make a tassel of the wool on the end. The result? A pretty, useful bookmark.

Cut the front of cards to postcard size, being sure to center the picture or design. On the reverse side of the picture, type "Message" and "Address" and separate the two sides with a ruled line, just as on a regular postcard. This is a great idea for making inexpensive Christmas postcards out of cards you've received over the years. You not only save money on the cards, but they cost less to mail than conventional letter-type cards.

Greeting cards can be made into attractive place mats. For each mat, cut two sheets of clear adhesive-backed plastic in the desired shape and size and seal an attractive grouping of the cards between the two sheets.

Cut out pictures from greeting cards and tie them into a colorful mobile for baby's nursery.

Jigsaw puzzles

Cover appropriately sized jigsaw puzzles with clean adhesive-backed plastic to use for place mats.

Mesh fruit bags

These are the bags that oranges, onions and other fruits and vegetables often come in.

Cut them into large pieces, bunch each piece up and secure with a rubber band to make net pot scrubbers that we all love to use on nonstick pans, while cleaning the bathroom and for numerous other cleaning chores.

Fill mesh bags with bread scraps, popcorn, suet and seeds to make bird feeders. If the mesh is very fine, cut out a few holes to allow the birds easy access to the food.

Mesh bags are ideal for moving yard plants. The large clump of "home" soil around the plant can be easily moved and relocated by replanting with the mesh bag intact.

Work a length of heavy wire through the mesh at the top of the bag, bend into a circle and twist the ends of the wire together to make a fishing net. Leave the ends of the wire long enough to twist together for a handle. This is a good project for children to make and use.

Use mesh bags to hold children's bathtub toys. Hang the bag over the faucet or shower bar. The toys will drip-dry after each use, will not mildew, and are less likely to be lost.

Plastic bags   Every trip to the grocery store will net you a fresh supply of plastic bags of all sizes. Save them all—plastic bread bags, produce bags, dry-cleaning bags, and purchased food storage bags. Of course you know you can use them for any number of storage purposes. Try them out as well for any of the following:

Keep a supply of plastic bags in baby's diaper bag to use for soiled diapers.

Sturdy plastic bags make adequate substitutes for rubber gloves when working with hair dyes or other mild but irritating chemicals. Be sure not to use with anything strong enough to dissolve the plastic.

Use plastic bags as inexpensive covers for kitchen appliances like the mixer, toaster or blender.

Cut bags into one-inch strips and crochet them into pretty, durable floor mats.

For camping or outdoor use, put pillows in plastic laundry bags, then cover with a zippered pillow case. The pillows stay fresh and dry.

Slip your hand into a plastic bag when greasing pans or mixing meatloaf.

Slipped over your shoes and secured with a shoelace or rubber band at the ankle, large plastic bags make serviceable emergency boots.

Have children slip plastic bags over their shoes before pulling on rubber boots. Boots will slide on easily.

Slipped over your socks before putting on shoes or boots, plastic bags will keep your feet warmer and drier in cold, wet or snowy weather.

Bread bags can be cut down to make sandwich-size bags. They can also be slit open as a free substitute for expensive plastic food wrap.

Line a bowl or small pan with a plastic bag when cleaning fruits or vegetables. Then just toss bag into the garbage can without making a soggy mess.

A large plastic dry-cleaner's bag or garbage bag makes a good emergency raincoat. Cut a hole in the bottom of the bag for your head and a slit in each side for your arms. Keep these on hand for guests who must venture home in unexpected wet weather.

Plastic lids   Even without the cans or containers they come with, plastic lids have many uses. They make perfect coasters under potted plants, candleholders, beverage glasses and opened oil and salad dressing bottles on the kitchen shelf to catch runny drips.

Cut the plastic lid from a coffee can or margarine container in half to make a perfect bowl, plate and pastry board scraper.

An easy way to make hamburger patties is to line a plastic lid with waxed paper or plastic wrap and pack the ground meat into this mold. The hamburger is easily removed by pulling up the food wrap, the patties are uniform in size and there's no mess.

The caps off soda bottles make good miniature paint pans for children to use with their watercolors. Just throw the caps away when they're finished.

The caps from toothpaste tubes are good substitutes for lost playing pieces in board games.

Plastic lids also make handy disposable cutting boards for smelly foods like onions.

Plastic shower curtains

Save these for handy drop cloths when painting or for using as a picnic cloth—either on the picnic table or to spread out on the ground.

Sheets and blankets

Worn fitted sheets can be used as mattress and box-spring covers.

Percale sheets make excellent lint-free dish towels for glassware and fine china.

Worn pillowcases can be used as dust covers on clothing. Just cut a small hole in the seamed end to slip the hanger hook through.

Use old flat sheets folded in half as a mattress pad.

Baby blankets can be sewn together (six or eight of them) to make a colorful patchwork blanket. This makes a nice keepsake for grandparents.

Transform a worn blanket into a fresh new-looking quilt, using two sheets as a cover. Sew one sheet to the blanket, then place the second sheet on top of the first (right sides together) and stitch around three sides. Turn right side out and hand stitch or bind the open end. To finish, quilt by making three or four lines of machine stitching evenly spaced down the length of all three layers, or tie a few quilting knots through the layers.

When electric blankets will no longer operate, they can continue to service as soft, warm, safe blankets by removing all the electric wires. Snip a very small hole where the wires are located and pull the wires out through the hole. Do this in several places—along the foot and on the underside. After the wiring is removed, take a needle and thread and whip the holes together. They will not be very noticeable after the blanket is washed and fluff dried and the blanket will be useful for many more years.

Socks and Hose

Thirteen ways to use old socks and nylon hose

1. Save the ribbed tops to make replacement jacket cuffs, or cuffs on children's knit shirts or pajamas when the sleeves become too short.

2. Cut old socks open, remove the toe areas and sew two together to make dusters, dish cloths and washcloths.

3. Wear a heavy pair of old socks *over* shoes or boots to prevent slipping on icy streets.

4. Use otherwise good socks with worn toes to make mittens. Cut a paper pattern of a mitten in the desired size and lay it on the sock so the ribbing on the sock becomes the wrist of the mitten. Cut out and stitch the outer edges with either straight or zigzag stitches. These make good liners to provide extra warmth to other mittens.

5. Save old socks to use as shoe bags when traveling.

6. A discarded sock slipped over a fly swatter is great for dusting under furniture and for reaching hard-to-reach places.

7. Save the tops from cotton crew socks to use as wrist bands to wear while washing walls and windows. They'll keep the water from running down your arms when you reach up over your head. You can also use these as sweat bands while jogging or exercising.

8. Use an old sock with the toe cut off to slip over a bandaged arm or leg at night to keep the bandage in place and protect bedsheets from bloodstains.

9. Knee socks make good arm warmers. Cut off the feet and slip the tubes over your arms to add a layer of warmth. This is especially helpful for arthritis sufferers or others whose elbows are particularly affected by cold.

10. Use strips of cut-up nylon hose to tie climbing plants to stakes in pots or the garden.

11. Support hose is good to use as a stretch bandage.

12. An old nylon put over a hairbrush will keep both the brush and your hair cleaner.

13. Elastic waistbands from pantyhose (and men's briefs) make good giant-size rubber bands for large boxes, etc.

Stamps

An old child's stamp collection (not a valuable one) can be put to decorative use by using the stamps to cover an old lamp shade. Glue the stamps on with white glue to completely cover the shade, allow to dry, then apply a coat of clear lacquer.

Stuffed toys

Outgrown small stuffed animals can be transformed into pin cushions that would be very appropriate gifts for grandparents. Glue the toy to a styrofoam base (which can be covered with fabric if you wish) and stick pins and needles into the body and head.

Table linens

Cut old linen tablecoths into lint-free dish cloths.

Cut plastic place mats into attractive beverage coasters.

Put pretty plastic place mats on your refrigerator shelves to protect them from spills.

When towels become old and worn, they still can be put to **Towels** good use. Try one of these money-savers.

A large old bath towel can be folded in half, stitched around the edges and used for a bath mat.

The sides and ends of large bath towels that have worn centers can be used to make wash or dish cloths. The edges can be zigzag stitched on the sewing machine.

Use the best parts of a worn bath towel to make a bag or mitt to hold worn soap slivers.

Many old towels still have a usable section large enough to make kitchen aprons. Rehem the piece and simply string a cord through the top hem for a tie.

Washcloths usually wear out in the middle first, while the outer edges are still good. Recycle them by cutting down the middle and sewing the outer edges together. Hem the new edges (formerly the middle) on two sides.

Index